Make Money from Your Writing

Aber Creative Writing Guides

Ghostwriting

Kate Walker's 12 Point Guide to Writing Romance

Starting to Write

The Craft of Fiction

Writing and Imagery

Writing Crime Fiction

Writing Historical Fiction

Writing How to Articles and Books

Writing Science Fiction

Writing Soap

Writing TV Scripts

Aber Self-Help

Choose Happiness: Ten Steps to Put the Magic Back
into your Life

Write yourself well: How writing therapy can help to
cure emotional and physical pain

Aber Money Management

Understanding the numbers: the first steps in
managing your money

Back to the Black: How to get out of Debt and Stay out
of Debt

Aber publishing

Make Money from Your Writing

Patrick Forsyth

www.aber-publishing.co.uk

Disclaimer

The advice given in this book is given in good faith. However readers are advised, where appropriate, to obtain the services of suitably qualified professionals for advice, particularly when pertaining to legal matters. Neither the author nor the publisher nor any/all of its agents can be held responsible for any outcomes that result from the reading of this book.

Typeset by Medlar Publishing Solutions
Printed and bound by Akcent Media

Dedication

For all those friends and colleagues in writing groups who have unfailingly encouraged my writing whilst daring to voice occasional (constructive and well founded) criticism; thanks to you all.

Success doesn't come to you... you go to it.

Marva Collins

Contents

9 An on-going process—keep thinking 105

Top tips and practical, proven ways to make your writing profitable

Writing can be fun, satisfying and, sometimes, profitable too. Writing may be difficult, and certainly it must be sufficiently good to deserve publication, but making money from your writing is another dimension: it does not just happen. You need to work at it. You need to do the right things in the right way in a systematic manner. But it is possible, both to do the right things in a manageable way and to see some cheques at the end of it.

This book reviews a plethora of money making action. It shows you how to regard writing in a business like way, how you can appeal to those, editors and others, who are potentially your customers and, above all, how you can permeate your whole approach with action specifically designed to maximise your chances of earning some useful money from your efforts. Whether writing is your hobby, a part-time or full-time activity, there are ideas here that will help you:

- organise how you work.
- present a powerful profile to your customers.
- increase your strike rate and your earnings.

The tenure of the book is realistic and practical, ideas and approaches are tried and tested and the focus is on action that can make a difference; it provides a positive catalyst to help you make a profitable difference to your writing and your life.

The author

Given the subject of this book, perhaps it is appropriate to start by setting out some author credentials; or would it be more impressive if this was my first book? It's not. With a background in marketing, time spent working in publishing and then a career primarily in management consultancy and training, writing has grown as an element of my portfolio of work over some years. While the great novel remains in limbo, I have had more than 100 non-fiction books published by some 20 or more publishers in the U.K. and overseas, and have translations published in 24 different languages. These range from a weighty textbook, written in collaboration with two academics (never again, they were many months late with their share of the text), through to hardbacks, paperbacks and a few slim monographs.

I have also edited books, co-written books and ghost written books, and spent time seeing all these through from manuscript to finished book; and helping support them in the market has seen me writing articles, giving interviews and appearing (occasionally) on radio. Oh, and surreptitiously moving copies to more conspicuous positions in bookshops.

In addition, I have written innumerable articles, undertaken copywriting and also penned pieces for a range of media including corporate publications and the now ubiquitous website.

So, I am well used to the process: contacting publishers, making suggestions, liaising over publication and promotion and I like to think that, over the years, I have had a reasonably good strike rate.

I have been a member of three different writing groups (and still attend such meetings) and have been a guest speaker at a variety of events ranging from small local writers' groups to the Society of Woman Writers and Journalists and the Singapore Writers' Festival.

I have written regularly for *Writing Magazine* for some years and certain of my previous books have touched on writing. These include: *How to write reports and proposals* (Kogan Page) and, more recently, *Empty when half full*, a humorous rant about the poor, mistaken and misleading communication aimed at us all as consumers (it worries me that an insecticide claims "... kills mosquitoes for up to 10 hours". They are surely going to be angry when they revive, and how…).

This is, however, the first time I have shared my observations and experience of writing work in this way and I am grateful to Aber Publishing for the opportunity and pleased to do so.

Patrick Forsyth
(www.patrickforsyth.com)

1 Introduction

No man but a blockhead ever wrote, except for money.
Samuel Johnson

So you want to earn some money from your writing. Or maybe you earn some already and want to earn more. First let's set out the bad news clearly: it is never easy so to do and it can be downright difficult.

But do not let that put you off. The good news is that it is possible and, what is more, there are ways of going about it that make it more likely to happen. I know, and I have had to learn the hard way. There are always disappointments along the way, of course, and many a writer could wallpaper the bathroom with rejections, but many things—articles, books, web pages and more—*are* published and the authors do get paid. At one end of the spectrum are the likes of J K Rowling, who is in receipt of tens of millions of pounds, although it took many rejections before she succeeded in getting published. And at the other end of the scale are those getting a few pounds or a few hundred pounds now and then or, better still, regularly.

Let me declare my position. I am certainly not in the J K Rowling category (more's the pity), but I have been published regularly—more than 100 books and countless articles—for many years and earn a significant part of my income at the keyboard. Naturally my writing career has also left some deathless prose abandoned along the way; no matter, I like to think that my strike rate is okay. Certainly I am used to the process of putting bread on the waters, of liaising with editors of all descriptions and to the process that flows from agreement to commission and seeing something through to publication. I like to think I know something about how to make money from writing, indeed I have written regularly for a number of years for *Writing Magazine* about doing just that; in fact, as you will see, some of what is in these pages is drawn from my column there, "Going to Market". Hence this book; and, yes, before you ask, I am being paid to write it. But surely it would hardly have credibility otherwise.

Lots of things are difficult. If you want to juggle with flaming torches and avoid burning holes in the carpet then you must learn how to do it and you must practise. Writing is no different (though how to write well is beyond the brief here) and nor is getting published and getting paid. You have to work at it. It is said that there is one word that describes a writer without persistence—unpublished. And the same sentiment doubtless applies to being paid for publication. The process has many elements to it, beginning, of course, with writing something of sufficient quality and relevance to be published. Not least is the question of writing appropriate query letters, synopses and proposals and any other sort of suggestion; this book does not review those issues, though many others do, including *The Craft of Fiction* by Jonathan Falla in this series.

What we are concerned with here are three things:

- the attitude you must take to the process.
- the techniques that go with being a "writer for hire".
- the on-going, systematic process of thinking of new things to do that will produce writing work, and executing them effectively.

Not least I am aiming for this book to be a catalyst: a spur to you trying to—or trying harder to—earn something from your writing by understanding how the process works and going about all the things you must do effectively. It is unashamedly a miscellany in one sense and the contents range from chapters setting out the specifics of something you need to be able to do in some detail (like Chapter 7 about public speaking); to a few hundred words designed to put over one simple idea, albeit one that is proven, practical and which may be either used as is, or adapted to suit you. That said, let's see what the core hurdle we must jump looks like.

Impressing the editor

It is said that timing can be everything. It was ever thus: the best part of 3000 years ago the Greek poet, Hesiod said "... right timing is in all things the most important factor". For writers it certainly makes a difference with submissions. A suggestion, an article or even a book can be turned down more than once, yet finally, and sometimes quickly, be accepted. The initial turndowns did not (necessarily) mean it was bad; it may have just not been right for where it was sent or simply have arrived at a bad moment: at the wrong moment in a magazine's publishing cycle, just when a rush was on, or another similar suggestion had been accepted from someone else. I have ample personal proof of this and have even had pieces and books rejected then accepted later by the same editor (with, for the record, very minor alteration). The latter moment was just better for some reason.

You kind of know what is likely to be going on as your deathless prose arrives.

The editor clicks on her email. Twenty seven messages await and amongst several spam ones and the third demand to pay a long overdue bill, half are new, speculative submissions. She sighs and pushes her chair back. A cup of coffee seems indicated before any further action is taken. It's going to be a busy day: there are deadlines to meet, a press release to write, correspondence to answer and an expenses chit to complete: the one from last month. All she needs to find in her In Box is a batch of query letters, speculatively written articles and unknown writers telling her that "even the best thing since sliced bread is not as good as this", followed by a cliché ridden piece of junk that she would never publish in a complete new material famine.

She sips her coffee and drops two Alka-Seltzers into the half-empty glass of water that has sat on her desk since yesterday and winces at the noise they make. She turns back

3

to her In Box. Her head throbs from a late night. She tries to concentrate. She deletes the message demanding payment and then picks a submission at random. The covering letter is ungrammatical, it has not been spellchecked and starts with the words, "My friends all think this is great". She reads one more sentence but only while she delays deleting it until she has freed up her hand by putting her coffee cup down. These people are kidding themselves. That last one—Mary whatever her name was—will never be a writer; most likely she has trouble writing a note for the milkman. Forget it. What next? She selects another submission at random. The sender has looked up her name—good; but spelt it incorrectly—bad. They are asking whether an article on cycling holidays for senior citizens in Tuscany would suit her. No. It. Would. Not. It is difficult to think of anything less appropriate. What's the matter with these people? Don't they check anything? Don't they think? Even for a split second? What's the definition of a split second? The length of time between recognising that a submission is as likely to suit as a weak cup of coffee is to cure her hangover and pressing the "Delete" key. She congratulates herself on coining the definition and presses said key with aplomb. The next email describes an attachment as a "filler". Maybe there is one little something here she can use. But no, it's five long, dense pages in ten point type and the first paragraph puts her off; no make that the first sentence. Enough—she resolves not even to look at the rest and goes to lunch.

That is the maelstrom into which many writers imagine their work arriving. In fact imagination runs riot: that is the least of it; that is what qualifies as a good day and… no wonder the downstairs loo is papered with rejection slips. But actually, I exaggerate (I hope) and it is certainly not always like this. Achieving success may take time and it certainly takes persistence but editors *are* accepting some things all the time. There are magazines to fill and bookshelves to stock and no reason why, provided you write appropriate stuff, you should not get agreement to contribute to the process. So during that worrying period between sending something in to an editor and getting a reply, try to be optimistic: there is every chance it will not arrive on the day from hell described here, that it will be seriously considered and that you may well receive an acceptance and see it go into print.

Perhaps the moral here is to not do this sort of imagining after you have submitted something, but *before* you do so. You can do much worse than to imagine the cringe-making sound of those Alka-Seltzers dissolving; in fact assume that is the mood you have to lift, make what you send designed to do just that and success, and even a good strike rate, is always possible.

But you do not just want to be published; you want to get paid for what you write, so let's move on: the next chapter sets out the kind of overview I think you need to have of being a "writer for hire". Clarity about this is vital and quickly shows what the possibilities are and how you can create and take advantage of opportunities (though always remember the old saying: *the trouble with opportunities is that they are so often disguised—as hard work*).

> *Note:* this book is designed to be useful to a wide range of writers, not only in terms of the amount they do, but also with regard to exactly *what* they do. Thus sometimes the emphasis and ideas are best suited to those writing books, sometimes to those writing articles (or websites and such like). The principles overlap and I believe both sides benefit the other.

2 Core principles of writing for profit

> *I never write the word metropolis when I get paid the same for writing city.*
>
> Mark Twain

Writing must be viewed as a business; or at least it must if you are to maximise the money you aim to make from it. This need not be daunting, but certain things must be done right. This chapter provides an overview and sets out numbers of factors all of which are important to how you work and what you will achieve.

The first thing is to consider the opportunity that a writer can grasp. As I have written already, I am being paid to write this book. Make no mistake, I am pleased to be writing it, I shall enjoy writing it, I am grateful for the opportunity to pass on some advice and I shall take some pleasure in seeing the book in print. I also like to encourage other writers; and sometimes it is nice to do so in the form of a shove towards publication and payment. But, if I am honest, I do not regard the process of writing as complete until a cheque lands on the doormat; I like that too. There may well be a parallel here with the attitude you take.

You may share my liking for the cheques or wish that a proportion of what you did could produce some. Here I will look not at the task of getting published but at how you can view your writing as a money making process and how you handle that side of things. Because, trust me on this, it does not just happen!

What kind of writer are you with regard to money? There can be many levels of earnings involved. Three are worth spelling out. First, there are those who just do a little writing, the occasional article appears as does the occasional cheque. Secondly, there are those who do a little more to the extent that it provides a regular and useful side-line. And thirdly, there are those who earn all or part of their living by writing. Wherever you are on the scale, you no doubt want to maximise what you earn and handle the finances appropriately.

Sources of income

Sources of income can vary a good deal and the first step to maximising income is to assess the possibilities and see how they benefit, or might benefit, you. What you write affects this. Not everyone has published books, but let's start with that. The income from a book will come primarily from royalties. These are normally paid with some sort of advance up front (typically split so that some comes on signing a contract, some on the manuscript being delivered and approved, and some on publication), then, if the book sells in a way where the per book royalty exceeds the advance, you begin to receive further payments. It is possible that this goes on for some time and both assistance with promotion and initiatives to keep a book in print—by producing an updated version of a non-fiction book for instance—are well worthwhile. In addition money may come from overseas translations and from such schemes as the Public Lending Rights (PLR) and Authors' Licensing & Collecting Society (ALCS); the latter you need to register for—if you have not done so and they could help you, then do so at once. Additionally of course there can be the profit on copies you buy and resell personally; something you can aim to maximise.

Different sources of income are possible once something is in print (and this does not only apply to books). One potentially important one is talks. For instance, I give talks at writing groups and the like and also, some linked to two travel books I have had published, for a variety of bodies ranging from Women's Institutes to Rotary Clubs. Such assignments can both pay a fee and constitute an opportunity to sell books to attendees. Of course a cheque for £100—or

£1000!—is better than one for £25, but for the part-time writer small sums may be useful and don't forget how they add up: £25 a month is £300 in a year, and that sum every week would be £1300. It all mounts up.

If articles are your thing then there should be fees from them and more fees if you republish them in a different form or overseas. There are links here also. A book being published may give you the opportunity to earn from articles about it or articles on the same topic, and several articles published on one topic may be turned into further opportunities as you place yourself in a position of being regarded as an expert on something, making it easier to sell more articles. Some people also do well enough to count writing competition wins as a component of their income, indeed there are some competitions from which a truly significant amount can be won. (I have only ever won one, but the prize was attendance on a course worth some £500.)

You may of course write and get something published which pays you nothing. While many writers do not want to do this very often, it can be useful (or you may not care about payment and just want to see your name in print—and why not if you so wish?). For example, an article may plug a book, or a talk or something else that will earn you money. Or maybe you can negotiate an alternative to payment. For example, writing an article for nothing on condition that you are paid for a second one (two at half price for the editor, one fee for you), or that you get a free subscription for a year if it is a monthly magazine; this latter option may be useful for you and actually costs the magazine very little. A big advantage of free placement may be to extend your writing record, adding something to your Resume/CV, and because one thing can lead to another, this too can produce further income.

The precise situation that prevails always needs to be borne in mind, and some things can be less than life changing in financial terms but very useful and go beyond just a one-off event. An example will make this clear. A year or two back, while on holiday in Thailand, I took a scuba diving course (and after a scary moment or two at the outset, it was a wonderful experience). I sold an article about doing this to a magazine and the fee more than paid for the cost of taking the course. I subsequently sold two more articles and have included something about it in a book. The first article led to getting further articles into the same journal, indeed this became a monthly input until the magazine sadly folded. I was delighted to be able to put the cost of the diving course down against tax and made a total sum, which while not being substantial, was a useful little balance against the cost of the holiday. Every little helps, as they say. Indeed you might well take the view that just to cover costs on such a thing is worthwhile. And… the whole thing was fun too; and if you do not write, at least in part, to get some fun from it all, then you should! We will return to expenses, and tax, later in this chapter.

I am not meaning to underestimate the job of securing paid commissions, there are many articles and books looking at the detail of such things as how to write a synopsis, so let's leave that on one side here. I hope, however, that I am persuading you that earning money from writing is possible and also that, over and above the task of seeking commissions, the way you view the money making potential matters. You need to wear a "business hat" sometimes in tandem with your creative one; I hope I am not mixing my metaphors too much here; the point is that the two must go together.

Making an investment

The fact is that one of the first aspects of the financial side of writing involves the word investment. Forgive me, but I do smile to myself sometimes when I hear or read letters bemoaning the fact that, say, the cost of postage is so high. Yes it is and something like a manuscript may weigh a good bit, but realistically you have to prime the pumps. You cannot expect to receive cheques and create significant earnings without putting something in to get and keep the process flowing. It's like any other business. Importantly, by "significant", and here I mean significant *to you*, the overall level does not matter and it may pay the mortgage or just fuel the "holiday fund" a little. You have to post things, buy stationery and keep your computer up to scratch. You may also have to travel to events or meetings, belong to bodies such as a writing group, take an editor for a cup of coffee or even a meal and a whole lot more besides. Such activities should be regarded not so much as a cost but rather as an investment. You mail something aiming to earn something later from the initiative. You have to respect the way the business works for both writers and publishers, and you have to work the system rather than rail against it. Sometimes research adds more to the costs.

The possibilities of earning are considerable. But, as I wrote early on, it does not just happen, you need to work at it and then you need to plan, organise and manage the financial aspects of what you do well, in order to make the most of it. Whether you just want to help defray the cost of a trip or create a regular useful income, the principles are similar. You have to view it the right way and you have to work at it the right way. When you do, and when you get the whole thing right, you can look at your name in print, and as well as taking pride in a creative achievement, take pleasure in being rewarded to whatever degree for it. At best, the end result is you laughing all the way to the bank.

So far, the key steps towards making writing a business are:

1. resolve to adopt a business attitude.
2. decide the mix of your work portfolio.
3. assess the monetary possibilities.
4. assess the other possible rewards.
5. consider and plan the necessary investment.

Organising to make it work

Having aimed to persuade you that earning money from writing is possible and that doing so needs a business-like approach, it should already be clear that it does not just happen. Being business-like implies activity that takes some time, so let me continue by looking at the overall work involved. This essentially falls into three categories. Before I list them, do note that the first balance necessary here is between writing and whatever else makes up your life. Many writers work part-time at it, so you may have other work to fit in and family and other commitments too.

Regarding writing:

- firstly, there are the activities you need to undertake to prompt commissions. Time is money, as they say, so you want such things to be done efficiently (it also needs to be done *effectively* so as to create the greatest chance of a good strike rate). This may involve a variety of tasks, from research to making approaches and following those through. You need persistence here and must avoid the "feast and famine" trap: that is, doing nothing that might produce new work while you are busy writing to fulfil some commission. What is necessary is regular and systematic activity, and that needs organising if anything like a steady flow of work is to be forthcoming.

- secondly, you need time to do the writing that *is* commissioned. Here the key is productivity. If I throw away three drafts of an article and find the fourth is 400 words short of what is needed, the process will take too long and will hardly be economic. Accuracy in this sense is especially important for articles and the like. If you are in a position to spend several speculative years on a book that is another matter; maybe you do this in parallel with some fee earning or other work.

- thirdly, and we must be realistic here, you need some administration time. You have to order stationery, keep the computer off the sick list and you also need some time to manage the financial side of things. This goes somewhat further than typing and sending the occasional invoice. You need clear records. Maybe some sort of job sheet is helpful. I have a note about articles, showing word count, fee to be paid, delivery date and invoice date and must then, separately, work out what to say in them. Even when a commission is delivered you may need to plan and record ongoing activity: to prompt you to chase if payment is late, to make suggestions for further writing and even to file the published work when it appears (and as you may well know that could be months ahead).

An administrative foundation

An important part of the necessary admin is keeping a record of your expenses. This makes a significant difference to your "pay". Earn £1000—let's be optimistic—and you end up with that much less, tax paid out, but if you have expenses that reduce the tax then this puts more money in your pocket. If you earn little as yet, you still need to take note and whatever amount it is may go alongside other earnings; it is the total that counts. Whether you have a full or part-time job, or earn from freelance earnings made from non-writing activities, the expenses set against it can be valuable to you. I will mention also the question of VAT. Not everyone will want, or need, to get into that—but, maybe if you have other freelance activities, the VAT you can claim back on, say, the cost of a new printer is worth having and can make a significant difference. VATable or not, you need careful records and receipts. It might surprise you how many things can be charged in this way and what costs add up to; it's worth some thought.

For Non-UK readers, VAT is British Goods and Services Tax (G.S.T.). You will need to check the position where you live but it is usually the case that VAT/GST can be claimed back on goods and services required for a business.

A balance is important here. Getting work must be a priority as, unless you do that, there is no (paid) writing to do. But some juggling may in fact be necessary to keep everything moving forward together. One important record to keep is of contacts: a publisher, a magazine editor and so on. A contact sheet is useful and these days, of course, you can design one on screen and update it on your computer. Each sheet can list the contact details of the person or people involved and then include a chronological record of communications made in either direction. Such might include for instance: you making suggestions, sending a synopsis, them agreeing (let's be positive again), you submitting copy, them sending you the edition of the magazine with your article in, you sending a thank you, followed by another suggestion. If you use three columns you can list the date, what action took place as suggested above, and how it was done: letter, phone call, email and so on. The latter allows you to ring the changes a little in terms of method; remember how instantly an email can be deleted and forgotten. And the dates allow you to judge whether your frequency of contact is suitable: too much and you become annoying, too little and they forget you or fail to take you seriously.

An important aspect of such a contact sheet is that the last entry should not be a record, but rather a prompt. In other words, you always add as the last entry what you plan to do *next*. This means there is never too much of a gap. The timing of what you do next should be a matter of judgement. For example, as I write, say, the second article of a series of three, it may well be too early to suggest further ideas. But with the third one delivered, I may well judge it too far ahead to wait until it is published and decide it's a good moment to initiate contact with the editor about "what next?". You can link such contact sheets to your diary, paper or electronic, so that you get a specific action prompt on the day you plan to make contact. If circumstances change—you have something topical to suggest, for instance—then the planned action can be advanced and implemented sooner; it is a good idea to write this last entry in pencil so that you can change it.

Before you have too much to record, you have to get work confirmed. Some things, like articles are pretty straightforward, though if payment details are not made clear you need to ask. Specifically: is there payment, how much is the fee (and also what rights is this buying, which may be important if you want to sell the article again, for example overseas) and when exactly will it be paid? Payment can be made on delivery, more often on publication and sometimes on a set date some while later. And, yes, just ask. I am surprised by how many people seem to be reluctant to do this. You must be clear and you must expect things to be difficult or impossible to sort out after the event if they are not clarified initially. If you think there is a fee and an editor doesn't, or if you think it will be double last time's fee as you are going to write twice as many words, then misunderstandings can easily occur. For a book, you will be offered a contract. The first time, this can seem long and confusing. Take a moment over it. It may be worth comparing notes with a more experienced author (or asking a body like The Society of Authors which will "vet" contracts). On the one hand, you may just want to sign before they change their minds about publishing you. On the other, there may be things, perhaps more than you might think, to negotiate—a thought that is picked up in Chapter 4. Let's take one simple example here: consider the question of complimentary author copies of a book. The cost of a few more copies to a publisher is low—just the print cost—the usefulness to you is higher: you can sell them, get them displayed or use them to create reviews or news stories to prompt additional sales and revenue. If you approach such issues early on, before signing a contract, then you may be able to create benefits that run for the life of a book. Publishers will not be surprised by your posing some questions and suggestions here. You may not get everything you want, but you may do better for raising something.

An appropriate profile

A final point here is important. Publishers and editors don't want any hassle and thus like to deal with a "safe pair of hands". It can improve the way you are dealt with, including financially, if you can make them believe this is what you will be. For example, if you offer help with publicity, taking an initiative and organising specific things, then extra copies of your book may readily be forthcoming. Ultimately, your competence needs proving. Deliver with a capital D and the perception of you changes. So, articles must comply accurately with the required word count (books too: count this Mr Editor; it's spot on!). Delivery must be on time and preferably earlier, and manuscripts must be in manageable form and not present a publisher with a nightmare of copy-editing. Without a doubt, being truly professional about how you work as well as what and how you write makes obtaining repeat assignments easier and that reduces your costs, as canvassing speculatively takes time and money, and increases your revenue.

With something commissioned, written, delivered on time and the invoice sent, it may seem like time to relax. Not so: there is more to do. But first, let's highlight some additional key steps:

1. analyse and work the balance between different tasks.
2. keep clear records (including expenses).
3. monitor contact communications chronologically.
4. clarify (and negotiate if necessary) fees and terms.
5. deliver with a capital D.

Reaping the rewards

Once you have completed and delivered a commission and sent out an invoice, then you can set to and write something new. Wrong. There is more to do, either before you move on or in parallel with so doing. High on the list of what must happen is ensuring that you get paid. Even if everything was arranged as best it can be, getting the money in may need a nudge. Some things are automatic: you are unlikely to have to chase for PLR fees (mentioned earlier), they are paid at specific times of the year. Advance royalties can be delayed, indeed come to think of it one publisher is late with some of mine right now—but I will resist the temptation to name and shame here. Sometimes there can be reasons for delay, and it is usually sensible not to base your cash flow on payment of an advance being made on the button. Though many are good, some publishers are just late payers and so too are some magazine editors. In the current economy this is surely not surprising.

Some people will blatantly withhold payment until someone chases. That's how it is, so be businesslike about it. Always send an invoice. If appropriate, state on it what your trading terms are: *TERMS: payment should be made within 30 days* or whatever, or restate theirs. Always add the details of your bank. Many people find payments easier and cheaper direct into a bank and not having this information is a regular excuse for delay. If necessary, follow up and remind people. Be firm: after all you have a contractual arrangement with them, they do actually *expect* to pay—albeit eventually. Do not cry wolf. I once saw a company which sent eight, increasingly strident reminders to those owing them money and spoilt it completely by putting, in red type, on each and every one the heading, "Final demand". If delays get really bad, do not threaten action unless you are prepared to take it or you are instantly labelled a soft touch—*they never do any more*, they say to themselves as they postpone payment a little more. One tip—and don't laugh and reject this—when you have to telephone someone to chase a payment, make the call standing up. Really. It works: you will find it much easier to be assertive, and starting with something apologetic like, "I'm sorry to worry you, but I wonder if…" and peppering your call with the words "perhaps", "possibly" and "maybe" is not likely to have the desired effect. Try it.

Money matters

When payments arrive successfully, record them and link them to any targets you may have set. It is good to set a figure to aim at. It doesn't matter if you select £100 a month or £1000 a month; or more. Just saying you will achieve "as much as possible" does not prompt any action; it actually just becomes a self-fulfilling prophesy. A target can be related to action; you are motivated to chase up the next project if you are only half way to your target. This is good if your earnings from writing are just a side line; but it is vital if they actually help pay the mortgage. Because writing is primarily a solitary process, such measurement of success is nice as a way of rewarding yourself too. One important point should be mentioned. When you do get a worthwhile cheque, do remember that it may well be that you have to pay tax on it, if so, it is best not to spend it all on the day it arrives. It is prudent to keep such earnings separate: perhaps even in a separate bank account and regard some of it—a set percentage—as untouchable until the taxman calls.

There may be other financial matters that need managing on a regular basis. For example, if you are putting money into a private pension then that is probably best done regularly—and, looking at the newspapers, is certainly prudent if you do not want an impoverished old age. However you are going to use your earnings, it is worth labelling the sums involved so that various proportions are allocated as needs be: tax, pension, general income and expenditure or holiday fund and what one friend of mine calls "mad money" meaning cash set aside for an unashamed treat.

Whatever the level of your income, it will certainly fluctuate, and should you actually go freelance and swap a regular salary for what are inevitably erratic earnings, it can be something of a shock to the system. I have worked freelance for many years, but I can still remember this surprising and worrying me early on. Some months were good; some very good. But some months were bad and I have had some when not a single penny has gone into my bank account, something that can happen either because you are actually doing no work or—hopefully more often—because although you are doing some work, no payment is due currently. One small device I found useful (still do, let's be honest) is to monitor the quarters through the year. I may have the occasional bad month, but payments even out and I have never had a really poor quarter; this measure can help distract you from what may occasionally seem like disaster.

Moving forward

When a piece of writing, a book, article, whatever, has been delivered, approved and paid for then there is no better time for two areas of activity that can increase your profits. First is publicity. With a book the income you will receive, which may continue for several or even many years, will depend ultimately on how many copies are sold. You can influence this. You can help the publisher sell copies by working with them on promotional initiatives (a bookshop signing session or talk in a library are just two examples of such activity), and you can sell copies yourself, increasing royalties and making a margin on copies bought and resold. This is obviously an area of many possibilities and, as well as these needing organising, you may need to take personal action too: fine-tuning your public speaking skills for example. With a book, such action needs preplanning, and remember that a title is only new once (though hardback and paperback may give you two shots at things)—and thus newsy things like an interview on your local radio station are easiest to fix at that time.

Secondly, it is useful to suggest new things in the wake of success. Your book or article is published. You have proved to be a safe pair of hands. The editor is thinking well of you so now's the time to suggest something new you might do for them. It is actually safer for an editor to reuse someone used successfully already than to try a new writer. They want things to be easy and quick to fix and reliable in their out-turn. You can help them achieve this and increase your revenue into the bargain.

Finally, while the whole tenure of this chapter has been about making money, let's consider just a few more things. Money saved is money in your pocket, so first off the tax and expenses considerations mentioned earlier are important. Non-financial rewards can be useful and satisfying too. If you want to travel or attend an event (The Hay Festival, a training course or conference), then being able to do so and break even on the finances of the situation is itself satisfying and financially useful.

I double-checked with David Aquino (who runs the accountancy firm Berkeley Townsend) and knows about these things (he not only does a good job on my accounts, but has bought and read some of my books). I asked about prizes and was told that competition prizes *are* taxable. The only exception may be if a prize is "unsolicited". This means that if you enter a competition and win something, that is taxable, but possibly if something you wrote collects an award without your chasing it, then it could escape (there have been some test cases here). With expenses you must be able to show that, in the words of the revenue, while losses may be tolerated for a while, you must operate "with a view to making a profit" and spend a reasonable amount of time so doing (10 hours a week was mentioned). At its simplest, if you just sit at home and write then expenses can be low, so the potential for profit even on a restricted scale of operation is high. But this may not concern you too much. Many people write and earn little, but they enjoy it, and maybe that is the most important element.

So, you can make writing a successful business and also a satisfying one. Doing so may need working at, but that can be done and the rewards, to whatever level you need or find useful, can add a further dimension to the process. It is nice to see your name in print, but perhaps even better to get a cheque as a result too. Have a go: making writing a business can be fun and, who knows, maybe what you can earn will be significant—maybe considerable. You could surprise yourself! So remember, some more key issues to bear in mind are:

1. chase debtors promptly and firmly to get paid.
2. categorise and ring fence monies earned (for tax, etc.).
3. set yourself a target and monitor your progress towards it.
4. sell and promote onwards on the basis of success to date.
5. take satisfaction from any useful non-financial rewards too.

A special source

There are various writing magazines and these can be a source of information, inspiration and more about writing, but only one, the best in my view, is also a source of market intelligence: news of publishers, people and publishing requirements, competitions and much more. It really can help you make money. Indeed, my writing this book followed my contacting the publisher having seen a note about them in the *Writers' News* pages. And that's *Writing Magazine*. I know I'm prejudiced because I write for it, but I believe it's true, and so too does the editor, Jonathan Telfer, so let's let him have his say too. He told me:

> "*Writing Magazine* is the UK's leading writing title. We aim to help writers of all kinds, at all levels, and in any genre, to be the best writers they can be.

To that end, in addition to our magazine articles, we run an extensive competition programme, interact heavily with writers through Twitter, Facebook and other social networking sites, our own website, www.writers-online.co.uk and the very popular online forum, Talkback... as well as answering direct queries if we have time.

The magazine itself has evolved quite a bit over the years. *Writers' News* was launched in 1989, followed a couple of years later by *Writing Magazine*. *Writers' News* featured publishing news, opportunities for writers, markets to sell your work, the latest publication news from our subscribers and other newsy titbits, and ran as a sister title to *Writing Magazine* for many years, before we decided to merge the two, early in 2011. So now *Writing Magazine* is fatter than it's ever been, 112 pages each month at least, incorporating all the news content of WN, and advice from professional writers on everything from shaping a poem to pitching a biography.

I've been with the magazines since 2001, and the special relationship we have with our readers has always thrilled me. It's great to be able to help writers directly, and even better when they call to let me know we suggested the opportunity to get them into print, or the new approach that gave them a breakthrough with Chapter 11."

In my view the advice is simple: no one who is serious about making any sort of money from writing should fail to read this excellent magazine. If you do not have a subscription, then I suggest you put that right soon. And don't forget to list it on your expenses.

Right, this chapter's finished: check word count, press save, work out what this many words have earned so far (a bit of self-motivation never goes amiss) and consider what needs to be in the next chapter.

3 **The not so gentle art of persuasion**

You need to be persuasive to succeed. Fact: writing commissions rarely simply fall into your lap. You have to actively win them (though repeat assignments may come a little more easily). And you may have to overcome a personal distaste for selling to do so. After all, you probably don't want to write in order to sell things and the archetypal image of, say a pushy double glazing salesman, is not entirely positive. The good news is that the individual techniques of selling, these being only the process of persuasive communication, are pretty much common sense. They are understandable. They are manageable (at least with practice). You *can* do it successfully. What is more, doing so can engender considerable satisfaction. It is always good to obtain a new customer. It is better still when you can look back and say *I made that happen.* So let's review how you can communicate persuasively.

Any complexity in selling comes from the fact that there are many different factors in play; and many different techniques to deploy also. The trick is in their coordination and appropriate deployment. Successful selling is dependent on several factors:

- understanding how the process works, and how the techniques can be used.
- deploying the appropriate techniques.
- focusing on the other person.
- communicating clearly.
- directing the interaction.

All these issues are investigated here to help you get to grips with the psychology involved.

What is selling?

Selling is part of your overall marketing or promotional activity. It is a process. A timescale is involved which may be short or long (sometimes months or even years). The full range of the activity spans such tasks as "prospecting" (making sure you have enough potential customers to talk to, for example those whose style matches yours and pay a reasonable rate), and "customer relationship management" (acting to make sure customers buy again and increase their business). Here we will concentrate on the process of securing work from someone who is expressing some interest—though you may well have sparked that interest.

You need to recognise that:

- it is natural for you and, say, an editor to have different perspectives (they want good quality or service and the best possible value for money in terms of what they get from you; you want a cheque and preferably soon).
- selling acts on a buyer to influence their decision.
- your job is to make your case clear, attractive and credible.
- you do so in a competitive environment; often someone is considering options in parallel from other writers, sometimes legions of them.
- part of your job, therefore, is to differentiate yourself from what is effectively competition.
- the process involves selling yourself, in the sense that the buyer must trust you and come to value your opinion.
- *how* you go about it is as important as *what* you do.

If you are knowledgeable about the way editors view matters, how they work and about the process of selling you must engage in, this knowledge gives you confidence. This is turn communicates itself to others—it is read as professionalism. Everything you do is predicated on this fact. Knowledge is power; certainly in selling, a lack of knowledge is fatal. For example, you know yourself that when you are buying something (a television, say), then any display of poor knowledge by whoever serves you in a shop rapidly knocks your confidence in everything that is being said to you.

Definition: the following may seem simplistic, but it provides a solid foundation to make everything you do in selling easier: *selling is helping people to buy*. A decision must be made. Your job is to help people do so, and—as you do so—to ensure they opt for your own proposition.

The buying decision

Consider. How do you decide to buy something? You review the choice—to consider an everyday product, let's say a new car—an initial filtering of possibilities quickly produces a shortlist. You decide to investigate a number of medium-sized hatchbacks. What next?

You want to know something about them:

- *the good points*: sensible petrol consumption, aspects of performance, styling and safety features such as ABS brakes. There is a complex list of considerations.
- *the less good points*: maybe such things as high insurance costs or higher than average depreciation. Again there may be a number of points.
- *the organisation*: in this case, both the manufacturer and the distributor. Are they reliable? What would happen if some fault were to appear? Here again, there may be a profusion of points good and bad.

Your decision is made having *weighed up* this balance. You want the case to be good. But you may compromise: selecting the sporty model despite the high insurance, say. You do not expect there to be *no* snags, certainly there are likely to be minor ones. You select the overall package that appeals, that provides value for money and—above all—that meets your needs.

This is exactly what people do with you. Your job is to help them. Usually a decision *will be made*, the question is when and with whom the work will be placed. You can influence both factors.

What this needs is a systematic approach. As we dissect the approach, and look at it stage-by-stage, remember that this is done only to produce familiarity that will ultimately enable you to run a seamless conversation—one which flows smoothly, does not seem to be being made up without thought, and which makes the prospect feel comfortable. *Note:* I suggest you imagine a conversation here. Of course much of your communication may need to be in writing, but essentially the same principles apply and you can do worse than regard written communication as a substitute for talking to someone.

Preparing to succeed

If there is any sort of magic formula about selling, it is here. Always do your homework: think about what you want to do before you do it. A plan should not be a straightjacket. Because you cannot ensure everything will go as you might like, it must be flexible. It is like a route map—useful when all is going to plan to keep you on the ideal route, but also useful to help change direction when something unforeseen happens.

So, spend a few minutes (it often need be no more) thinking through:

- what you are aiming at (clear objectives are essential).
- what you will do.
- what sequence you will use to present your case.
- how you will describe your case.
- whether anything is necessary to help the process (sales aids: anything to demonstrate your experience and style from a biographical note to examples of past writing).
- the likely response and questions that could be posed.

With this clearly in mind, you can proceed to the conversation with confidence.

Directing a sales meeting

1. Getting off to a good start

The initial moments of a meeting are disproportionately important (so too are the first words in writing). They set the scene for what is to come. The tone must be friendly yet professional and businesslike. Indeed, just being organised—in the sense of volunteering an agenda (one that will suit them)—can create the right sort of atmosphere. All you need at this stage is for people to think—*Yes, so far so good, this should be interesting.*

Other factors are important at this stage:

- *respect for time*: just ascertaining how long someone will give you can make the meeting easier; and sticking to time will always impress.
- *creating roles and rapport*: the buying/selling relationship needs setting up. You need to think about how you want to position yourself: as an expert, advisor—whatever.
- *discovering peoples' needs:* do not settle for superficial information. Ask and ask more. Use open questions, that is, those that cannot be answered by yes or no and which thus get the prospect talking. These typically begin with who, what, why, when, where and how: as in, "What readers should this feature appeal to?" Make it clear that you need to ask questions and that your understanding is in their interests. Note the growing information and how it paints a picture for you of what you are dealing with, and make sure that, as you proceed, you relate back to it, matching your comments to their requirements. This personalising of your case is vital to being persuasive— and differentiates you from competition (particularly those who have failed to discover as much).
- *linking neatly to making your case:* the early stages set the scene and allow you to move smoothly into making your case. Keep telling the prospect what you propose in terms that are customer-orientated—*right, I've a clear idea what you need, in light of the urgency perhaps it would help for*

*me to go through the timescale we would need. I think
you'll find I can hit that deadline.*

2. Presenting a persuasive case

This is the heartland of the dialogue. You must achieve
several intentions as you proceed:

- *make what you say clear:* this sounds obvious, but many
  sales fail only because someone is left unsure of what
  they are told. And sometimes a convoluted approach
  can compound the problems. Think about how you will
  explain things and make your message logical and easy to
  follow. You can score points here as people love it when
  something they expect to be complicated, turns out to be
  much easier than expected to follow.
- *make it descriptive:* paint a picture and do so with
  conviction. Never suggest something "quite nice" or "very
  good". Use adjectives. Relate one thing to another. Create
  a turn of phrase that gets to the core of what you want to
  put over.
- *make it attractive:* the prime method here is through what
  sales people call "talking benefits". Sales jargon defines
  features and *benefits. Features* are factual statements
  about something. *Benefits* are factors that do something
  for, or mean something to, the prospect. So saying that
  an article is 1500 words is a feature, saying that the detail
  you will set out will be sufficient for readers to do or
  learn something is a benefit; as the benefit of reading
  this chapter should be that readers will be able to make
  a more persuasive case having read it. In other words:
  benefits lead to and create a reason to buy; one that can
  be tailored to a particular person or publication. Features
  provide the reason why the benefit can be delivered.
- *build up a positive case:* point by point, you must spell
  out the advantages. Talking benefits, linking matters
  logically, explaining precisely and succinctly and giving
  as much detail as necessary. While comprehensiveness is
  never an objective, a full picture is, especially one that
  matches the customer's needs. Leaving out a key element

of the positive evidence, so to speak, can be dangerous. It dilutes your argument and, at worst, can do so to a level where a competitor seems a better bet.

- *add proof:* remember the prospect may understandably feel you have a vested interest in saying how good something is. Add *external* evidence—like a magazine getting many letters as a result of a feature you wrote—to reinforce your case.

Overall, the trick at this stage is to remain positive throughout and ensure you present a case that holds together neatly. It must not sound as if you are haphazardly making it up on the spur of the moment. It must sound considered and as if trouble is being taken to present things in a way that is right for the individual (which, of course, it should be). Referring to this will create a customer-focused feeling.

People should feel you see the meeting as "working with them", and certainly you should not come over as "doing something to them" in an unpleasant sense or putting your own interests first.

3. Keeping on track

Another job must be done at this point; indeed this may need attention throughout the piece. Remember that people are literally weighing things up. As you explain, they will form a view of what is good and less than good, as it were on a mental balance. You need to consider the snags.

Some will be raised—*that seems rather too many words.* Some *you* should raise (where you know they are likely to think of something and it will automatically become a negative if neither party raises it).

Answers do not necessarily have to demolish objections. Someone may, after all, have a point. You have to work to adjust the balance. There are only four possible courses of action, you can take:

- *remove the point from the balance:* sometimes a prospect is simply wrong, they have made an incorrect assumption or you have not made something clear. Put them right, but do so diplomatically.

- *reduce its significance:* here you agree—to an extent—but make clear no great harm is done.
- *turn it into something positive:* literally reverse their thinking—*actually this can be an advantage...*
- *agree it, but put it in perspective:* never fight an inevitable logic; you will just seem stupid (or desperate). If there is a downside, say so. You can minimise it, and in this—as in all the cases—discuss the point in the context of the whole balance and the advantages.

Dealing with objections one at a time, aiming to maintain a positive balance—and not appearing panicked—will keep the overall case positive.

4. Gaining a commitment

Finally, you need to "close" (sales jargon again), that is ask for a commitment. This does not cause people to buy—everything else you have done does that—but it can prompt action, turning the interest you have generated into action. This action may be to agree—to buy. Or it may be some other positive step along the way—agreeing that you send a sample or whatever. Whatever stage you are at needs this positive prompt.

Not explicitly closing negates your earlier good work. Checking is no substitute for a close. Ask—*Is that all the information you need at present?*—and you risk them ending matters (at least for the moment)—*Yes, that's been most helpful, let me think on it. I'll call you next week. Goodbye.*

Closing is not complicated, it must take place. You can:

- just ask—*Can we go ahead?*
- assume agreement and run the conversation on—*Fine, we seem agreed about it all, if you can confirm by email I'll...*
- offer alternatives—*Do you want A or B?* (ideally, with the first more specifically stated than the second, and with two more to offer if neither find favour).

You can check out more forms of close but beware of being too clever; it is, in any case, not usually necessary and can appear pushy.

Finishing off the process

No more may be necessary. If you get agreement, thank them, see to any administrative matters and end matters reasonably promptly (it is possible to ramble on and talk them out of it).

Or further action may be necessary, for instance:

- *delay:* they may say: *I'll think about it.* Always agree: *it's an important decision, of course you must be sure.* But find out why: *...but why particularly do you need to do this? Is anything still unclear?* This may unearth extra information. For example, that something *is* unclear (with clarification there and then allowing you to close again), or that the decision needs ratifying elsewhere. Always keep the initiative. Find out when a decision will be reached and volunteer to make contact again.

Action here may obtain agreement or lead to further stages:

- *be persistent:* keep in touch. Take every delay at face value. If someone says the buyer is out of the office when you telephone, call again. And again and again. It is their timing that matters and you can get orders by persevering after less persistent competitors have given up.

What matters is the success rate. No one wins them all. It may not always be as easy or quick as you would like but, if the techniques are well understood and appropriately deployed, you have every chance of being effective.

Selling goes with the territory. It is a necessary part of being in business as a writer. It will not just happen and few of us inherently have the qualities of the mythical "born salesperson". The secrets of success are to understand the process, planning ahead and making persuasive communication work for you. Here, because there is some complexity involved, I might also recommend my book *Persuasion* (published by Legend Press) and make the additional point that plugging is a useful form of selling!

Summary

Let me finish this chapter with some do's and don'ts:

- *make your case understandable*. First things first, no one will agree to anything they do not understand. And every time someone says: *I'm not quite sure what you* mean, they are not just clarifying one point they are adopting a view of someone who is unprofessional or unsure of themselves (and in writing they can't just ask, as they can face-to-face). Furthermore, utter clarity always impresses: a good, succinct description that gets people saying, *Seems straightforward so far* and wanting to hear more. Like any communication, a persuasive message needs organising, you need to go through things in a logical order in a way that, while factual and clear, also projects something of yourself. If you want to sound friendly, efficient, or professional—whatever, make sure such characteristics show. People agree most readily with those who seem to show that they are to be believed, who have the necessary knowledge and expertise.

- *avoid an introspective tone*, where every thought begins with the word *"I"—I will... I can... I offer...* and worst of all *I want*. It creates a "catalogue" feeling, listing things from your point of view; it becomes tedious and is unlikely to prompt interest. Try rephrasing any such sentiment starting with the word *"You"*. It will sound very different. Thus: *I would like to give you...* becomes something that begins *You will find...* If the latter continues by explaining *why* people will find something interesting or valuable, better still.

- *avoid circumspection*. A persuasive tone has no place for *I think—I hope—probably—maybe* or *perhaps*. Have the courage of your convictions. Anything for which you seek agreement, must reflect your confidence in it. So phrases like *this **will** give you...* are better. Similarly avoid bland description. As was said earlier, your case is never just *very good*. Nothing about your proposition should be stated as being *quite interesting*. Use words and descriptions that add drama and certitude. Attention here can transform a case. The job is to bring your ideas to life, to have people really wanting to hear more about them and recognising—easily and up front—that they are (if they are) special.

- *stress the benefits.* Remember: *features* are factual things—tangible or intangible—about something. An article may be c.1000 words long, occupy one page and deal with being persuasive or whatever: all these facts are features. Whereas *benefits* are things that something does for or means to people. So the benefits—that is, the results—of reading this chapter are things like: receiving an introduction to a useful aspect of persuasive communication; help in avoiding your making key mistakes that will dilute your persuasive effectiveness; or increasing the chances of your next proposal being accepted. Benefits should always predominate. They should be sufficient to persuade, they should be well expressed and lead the message rather than being tagged on as some sort of afterthought. Additionally, it is often necessary for a case to be backed up by proof or evidence. That is something other than *you* saying so. It includes everything from the opinions of others likely to be respected by whomever you aim to persuade, to factual evidence (so do not make the mistake of saying *all my friends like it*).

So, ensuring that you are persuasive needs some preparation. Think about what you want to say. Ask yourself why anyone should agree to your idea or proposal. List the reasons—all of them. Then organise them. What is most important? Arrange a logical argument: say something at the beginning to command attention and then ensure you maintain interest throughout. A powerful start quickly tailing away will persuade no one. Lead with the benefits. And let features follow to explain. This chapter will *allow readers to experiment with a more persuasive style* (benefit), because it is *written reflecting proven, practical approaches to communication* (feature). Then, when you do close—*ask for agreement*—doing so increases your chances of getting it.

4 **Negotiating the best deal**

If you want a guinea pig, you start by asking for a pony.

Annabel (aged 6), from the Internet

The last chapter made it clear that being persuasive adds a whole new dimension to the act of communicating (which is not always the easiest thing anyway), here we investigate briefly a close partner of persuasiveness, that of negotiating. Sometimes an offer of publication can be so overwhelmingly welcome that authors may sign up for anything. But there are deals and deals and, so far as is possible, you want to have publication arranged on the best possible basis.

Getting the best deal

There is an old saying that you don't get what you deserve, you get what you negotiate. True. Publication may be welcome, but perhaps not on any terms. A publishing arrangement is, remember, a contractual one and, while this may apply primarily to book publication, you do need to be clear what the exact arrangements are even for a "simple" article.

First you must regard the process of agreeing terms as negotiable. Consider something apparently simple— deadlines. Sometimes they seem fixed. A magazine may go to press on a particular day each month, miss that and your deathless prose is omitted. But maybe you can make the editor happy to have it in the following issue. A book manuscript must be delivered on time; a date you must be sure you can hit. Contracts usually run to many pages and deadlines are but one of their contents.

All such details are negotiable. But you need to know how to tackle what is essentially a complex process. Negotiation is bargaining to reach a mutually agreeable outcome.

Both parties must end it content (what is referred to as "win-win"). So it needs some thought. Good negotiators do their homework. They also respect the other party and work at understanding their position. That said, you must still be prepared to fight your corner, take time to do so and be patient; never rush negotiating or appear to be pushing for a swift conclusion—it will be seen as rushing to get your own way, and resisted. So how do you go about it?

Deploying the techniques

You need to be clear what you want (hence the need for some homework), particularly as this may relate to many different things. Everything is potentially variable: from deadlines and financial terms to the right of veto over, say, a book's cover design.

Topics for negotiation include:

- advances: their amount and timing.
- deadlines: for manuscript, proofs and publication (and method of delivery too—emailing a manuscript is cheapest for you).
- royalty rates (home and overseas; and, separately these days, electronic ones).
- subcontracting tasks (like indexing).
- publicity: what will be done, how much will be done and by whom.
- author involvement (in, say, cover design, advance reviews and publicity).
- overseas contract/sales arrangements.
- communication: who will liaise with who about what and when.
- particular initiatives (for example, will pre-publication reviews be sought using the manuscript, and if so, from and by whom).

You can doubtless think of more (list and prioritise what's important to you). Particular situations may add to the list (for example, in a magazine you may want your article in a special position). One detail agreed as *you* want, rather than left unaddressed, may make a project more successful.

This implies an assertive approach, yet one deployed with empathy and which avoids inappropriate confrontation. Do not get into a corner you cannot get out of. Avoid rows and showdowns, but stand firm and keep calm. Do not let perfection be the enemy of the good. An outcome that is 100 per cent what you want is rare. Be realistic; do not waste time and effort seeking an impossible ideal.

Use openness, but do so carefully. Declaring your plans and intentions may assist the discussion, but you may want to keep your underlying motivation hidden. Stick with your objectives, be watchful and, if necessary, bide your time (some things might best be discussed over several meetings or contacts). Always be professional: for example, always respect confidences given during negotiations. Such consideration builds relationships and may help you in future, for instance with an editor for whom you come to work regularly.

Finally, never underestimate people. And always end discussions positively; neither party will get exactly what they want, but if the deal is agreeable emphasise this at the end. If all this seems somewhat complicated, so be it. The complexities mean that the best negotiators keep a firm overview in their mind as discussions proceed.

The core principle

One thing about the process is of fundamental importance to success. You do not make demands, you *trade*—primarily through a process of "*If…* then". So: "*If* I could deliver on that day, *then* could you allow me a larger word count for the article, it's going to take much longer to write if it must be so brief?" Here you are giving something (delivery on the demanded date) but asking for something in return (a longer article: easier to write and paying a higher fee). And: "*If* I agreed that the advance is all paid on publication, rather than spilt between signing contracts, delivery of manuscript and publication, *then* perhaps the overall sum paid could be a little higher?" In using this technique you must minimise the value of what is given to you (*well, I suppose that helps a bit*) and maximise the value of what you offer (*this will really help the publication process and save money*).

Also, when there is a list of topics (terms) under discussion, try to identify someone's whole shopping list in advance so that you know what you are dealing with. Agreeing things progressively allows surprises to be sprung towards the end—*there's just one more minor point*, they say, raising something major.

Summarising the tactics

If persuasion is getting agreement to a course of action, then negotiation goes further: it obtains agreement to the way that agreement will be executed—the terms and conditions that will apply (the "variables" in the jargon). Much of what makes negotiation successful is in the details and in the sensitivity with which the process is approached. Given the dynamic nature of this complex interactive skill, let me summarise by reviewing ten key areas—some leading inevitably to others, others linking back to what has been said earlier—and, while not together being a panacea, they may help to highlight something of the nature of the process and the tactics that can make it work. The first is not only important, but also logically comes first.

1. Be prepared

With a process with the complexity of negotiation, it is not surprising that preparation is key. Early on it accelerates the value of experience and, beyond that, it acts to create a valuable foundation to the actual negotiation that follows. In one sense, preparation is no more than respect for the old premise that it is best to open your mind before you open your mouth. Such preparation must, of course, be combined with that approach for the whole meeting (or series of, say, emails).

Thus, preparation may consist of a few quiet minutes just before you step into a meeting. Alternatively, it may consist of sitting down for a while, perhaps with a colleague or friend, to clarify intentions and thrash out the best tactics to adopt—or everything in between. It can be stretched to include rehearsal, i.e. actually running through what you want to happen, rather as you might (sensibly) rehearse an important presentation. So:

- give preparation adequate time (in a hectic life, that also means starting far enough in advance).
- involve other people if that is possible and helpful.
- assemble and analyse the necessary information (and take key facts to the meeting, for example in negotiations involving money there may be calculations best pre-done).

Preparation should not assume that you can then guarantee everything will proceed exactly as planned. Planning is as much to help fine-tune what is being done when circumstances do take an unforeseen turn. Experience may reduce the time preparation takes; it does not however make it unnecessary. Remember, too, the saying attributed to a famous golfer: *The more that I practise my game, the more good luck I seem to have.* So, never skimp preparation in terms of time and effort. It is too late when you come out of a meeting that has not gone well saying—*If only I had…*

2. Communicate clearly

Like preparation, the best way to describe clear communication is as a foundation to success. Your communications— always important—need to be absolutely clear within a complex negotiation situation. Even an ill-considered word or two can destroy meaning or result in ambiguity; for example you still see signs saying, "Ears pierced while you wait"— implying that there is some other way of doing it? Examples of this sort of thing abound. There is a power that flows directly from sheer clarity and good description. When people:

- *understand*: this speaks for itself, but it also means misunderstandings are avoided and it helps ensure that the meeting stays tightly on its real agenda.

- *are impressed*: clarity gives favourable impressions of your authority, certainty and confidence—all of which add to the power you bring to the table.

Additionally, clarity about the meeting itself—setting a clear agenda and so on—directs the proceedings and helps make it possible for you to take a lead, which in turn helps get you where you want to go.

Clarity stems from preparation, clear thinking and analysis; and from experience. It is worth working at. The last thing you want at the end of the day is to achieve agreement, only to find it retracted later because someone says that *they were not clear what it was they were agreeing to*. Insisting at that stage can mean you are never trusted again; it is a position to avoid.

3. Look the part

This has already been flagged as important; certainly it can have a considerable effect on the outcome of negotiating. A sensible view of the literal aspect of this is clearly prudent: even in this informal age, you may need to be appropriately turned out. More important is that the profile you project gives specific impressions, for instance if you are seen as:

- *well prepared*, then people give what you say greater weight.
- *well organised*, this has a similar effect.
- *confident*, this can have a major impact on the credibility of what you say, especially the belief in your insistence that you *can do no more* if your arm is being twisted.
- *professional*, again a whole raft of characteristics may contribute to this from appearing experienced, expert or approachable to something like just appearing not to be rushed, and again the case you make will engender more consideration if the person making it is seen in the right light.

The point here is that something should be done to make any such characteristic more visible where this might help, and sometimes this might become a useful exaggeration.

In addition to what is said, many judgements come from visual signals and it is wise therefore to use them. Thus, for example, a display of attention to detail when faced with someone wanting to dot every i is useful.

4. Respect other people

Negotiation is a cut and thrust process. It certainly has an *adversarial* aspect to it and everyone involved is very much aware of this. While it may be important to take a tough line, to be firm and to insist, this is always more acceptable if the overall tenure of a meeting is kept essentially courteous.

Show that you understand other peoples' points of view. Be seen to find out what they are, to note details that are important to them and to refer to this during the meeting—"you said earlier…". Be prepared to apologise, to flatter, to ask opinions and to show respect (in some cases perhaps, whether you feel it is deserved or not!).

Apart from wanting to maintain normal courtesies in what can sometimes be a difficult situation, showing respect can help your case. If you have to take a strong line, there is a danger that it can be seen simply as an unreasonable attack; if it is taken that way, then the automatic response is a rebuff. If the strong line comes from someone who is clearly expressing respect for others and their views, then it is more likely to be taken seriously, considered and perhaps agreed.

5. Aim High

This is undoubtedly the most important technique involved. Indeed it conditions much about your whole approach. Aim high. Start by considering, in your planning, what this means. Think about what might be possible, think about what would really be best for you—and go for that. Remember that there is, no doubt, a list of variables—perhaps a long list—and that what you hope to agree is a mix of them all. Variables are the factors—the terms and conditions as it were—to be negotiated (with articles, two factors might be the deadline for delivery and the word count). Essentially the process here is to trade them on an "if I agree to make it 2000 words, will you allow delivery a week later" basis. Consider what the best position in all areas is—and go for that.

Negotiation is about to and fro argument, and about compromise, but it is very easy for compromise to become a foregone conclusion. You can always trade down from an initial stance, but it is very difficult to trade up. Once a meeting is underway and your starting point is on the table, you cannot offer another starting point.

Starting as you mean to go on is an inherent part of aiming high.

6. Get their shopping list

This rule links to the fact that you need to negotiate a package. If you agree parts of a deal individually, then you reduce your ability to vary the package because more and more of it becomes fixed. Something may seem straightforward in isolation. You are happy to agree it, yet suddenly you come to other points that you want to negotiate about, and there is nothing left with which to trade.

The principle here is simple. You need to find out the full list of what the other party needs to agree. Then you must not allow parts, possibly in fact important parts, to be picked off and secured one at a time, as a preliminary to hitting you with major demands at a stage where your options are limited.

7. Keep searching for variables

Variables can be listed as part of your preparation; listed and prioritised. Even a thorough job at this stage can leave things out. *Everything* is negotiable, *everything* is potentially a variable—and this includes things that have specifically been excluded by one party or the other. You may have said something—a deadline perhaps—is unchangeable and then decide that you need the additional power that agreeing to shift a little would give you.

Certainly you need to question what the other party means. Does—*That's it, I definitely cannot go any further on this*—mean what it says, or only that someone hopes they will not need to negotiate further about something? Questions, or a challenge, may be necessary to find out. The search for possible variables and different mixes in their respective priority must continue throughout the whole process. As the process demands more compromise from someone, then they may have to accept that things they hoped could be regarded as fixed will have to be regarded as variables. And that some variables may need to be more variable than was the original intention.

Preparing a list in your mind (or noted down) helps—if you are arranging details even about something as straightforward as an article you may need to deal with: style (make it humorous or not, say), length (word count), delivery date, embellishments (such as a boxed check list at the end, for a how-to-type article), illustrations (are there any and what sort—photos, diagrams etc.), fee (and payment terms: on publication or whatever)—it is easy at the end of a conversation to find something has been left unused or not agreed.

Keep an open mind, keep searching and assume everything is always a potential variable.

8. Utilise the techniques

Your success in negotiations is less likely to come from a single clever ploy or one display of power. It comes through the details. There is much to keep in mind during a negotiation, and the situation becomes more complicated as negotiations proceed. You can influence matters in a hundred different ways, but they need to be appropriate ways.

The good negotiator deploys a range of techniques (more of this in the next section), so they need to be familiar with them and able to make the best use of them. But it is not a question of blasting the other party with a hail of techniques; they need using with surgical precision. You must know just when it is appropriate to be silent, or to show that you are truly adamant.

Negotiation must never be allowed to take place on "automatic pilot". Every move must be considered, and this applies as much to *how* you do things as to *what* you do. Techniques (both overall, like the trading of variables, and in terms of smaller ones noted below) must be made to work for you and the way to do this is on a case-by-case basis—one that reflects what is right for this person, this meeting and this moment of this meeting.

9. Manage and control the process

Certainly overall orchestration is a major issue. It is all too easy to find that the concentration that is necessary to deal with the immediate situation can result in your taking your eye off the ball in terms of the total game plan.

You need to take every possible action to help yourself stand back and work with the full picture. For example:

- make notes.
- summarise regularly to recap (and *always* do so if you feel yourself getting lost; you do not need to say why).
- keep as much of an eye on the broad picture as on the needs of the moment.
- keep your objectives and the desired outcome clearly in mind.
- be prepared to take whatever action is necessary to keep on top of the situation (e.g. to pause and take stock) despite how you think it may look (in fact such action almost always simply increases the level of confidence you project).

If you approach this aspect of the process consciously, note what helps you, and allow positive habits to become established, then your experience and competence will build positively and quickly.

10. Be forever on your guard

Never relax for a single second. Even when things are going well, when events seem to be following your plan accurately, when one agreement is following another—be wary. Do not relax your attempts to read between the lines in such circumstances and do not assume that the positive path will continue. If you assume anything at all, assume that there is danger, reversal or surprise just round the corner and be ready for it; this is actually a pretty good philosophy whatever kind of meeting you are in.

Remember that *both* parties are doing their best to meet their own objectives and that the other person is just as likely to be playing a long game as to be a pushover. It is not over until it is over, and it is often late in the day that things come out of the woodwork and change what looked like, until that moment, a straightforward agreement.

Finally under this last heading, remember the words accredited to Lord Hore-Belisha: *When a man tells me he is going to put all his cards on the table, I always look up his sleeve*. It is good advice. Similarly when contractual matters are involved, as they usually are in negotiations (and other sorts of meeting for that matter), remember the saying—*The big print giveth, and the fine print taketh away* (J. Fulton Sheen).

By focusing on the ten points above it is not intended to imply the process is more complicated than it is; it can be, but then again such a discussion may only take ten minutes. Even so, the details always matter. The first step to making it work is to understand the principles and to adopt something of the techniques and how to deploy them. With that in mind, you need a conscious approach so that you make your experience build fast, and then note what works well for you, using it to strengthen your future ability to get the deal you want when a meeting demands it... or when faced with a youngster wanting a guinea pig!

5 Dealing with publishers

> *A writer is someone for whom writing is more difficult than it is for other people.*
>
> Thomas Mann

Whatever you write, publishers want "low-hassle writers". As was said in Chapter 2, they want you to deliver and deliver with a capital D. Thus, on the one hand you need to work with people primarily as suits them. You want to stay in touch, certainly to enable you to get one commission secured and to sell on suggesting more; but you can all too easily become a nuisance and get categorized as someone to avoid, at least to some extent.

It is a fine line, but on the other hand publishers want a safe pair of hands. This view may be drawn quite quickly. For instance, I recently had an exchange of brief emails with a publisher about the possibility of a book. It looked, I thought, promising but contact was superficial and brief. Then the phone rang. The editor had been looking me up on line, my website, and perhaps others I am featured on, and suddenly the tenure of the contact changed. He had jumped forward to seeing me as very likely to be a safe pair of hands and the conversation moved forward and a contract followed. This was at the beginning of a new relationship, but the same is true more gradually over time—an editor's experience of working with you must give the right impression. And then, from a solid basis of mutual respect, you can work the process and communicate in a way that puts bread on the waters for the future.

A good relationship with an editor should not be taken for granted; it must be actively earned. So let's take that as a starting point and look at overall things about the relationship first.

So you have a contract (and if not—*imagine*; let us be positive). Writing then becomes a prime preoccupation, but you also need to think ahead: you have a publisher and you need to think about how to relate to them. You need to think about what they expect of you.

Your editor

First things first: you must deliver on time, and preferably a little ahead of time. Never, ever agree a deadline you are not confident of hitting. If the worst happens and you are going to be late, the next best thing is to give some warning and a reliable alternative date. Anything less, especially missed fall-back deadlines and implausible excuses, and you risk creating a bad reputation. Such can quickly spread widely within a publishing company, as witch-hunts into delays involve many people. With books, never forget that the long sequence of actions flowing from signature of contract to publication and launch make any variance a real problem for the publisher. It is true that a missed deadline could see you never asked to do anything again.

Other things link closely to this. Sheldon Press publish primarily self-help books (including some with wonderful titles such as *How to love a difficult man*). Joanna Moriarty, their Editorial Director, has—like most editors—firm views about what constitutes a good author (and many others I have dealt with say similar things). Beyond hitting deadlines, she comments, "Writing to the prescribed extent is crucial—cutting is much more painful (for all parties) than getting it right first time. You may honestly believe that the extra 40,000 words makes it a far better book, but the project will have been signed up on the basis of a detailed costing and project specification, and such changes can seriously compromise its viability. And cutting leads to delays and schedule slippages."

Reflecting reality

She also feels authors should be aware of the whole team that is behind the production of their book. "Expressing appreciation of the work of the people who handle copy-editing and proofreading is always a good thing, though phoning the Production Department probably never is," she says. Overall, authors must be realistic about the nature of the real world of publishing and that means understanding how it all works—perhaps reading up on this should be part of any author's basic research: check out *Inside Book Publishing* (Routledge). Not least, this realism must relate to financial issues. For most authors, the much-publicised six-figure advance awarded to someone like Martin Amis has little bearing on their own negotiations, though it is always good to have a comma in your royalty figures.

This sort of realism must infect all aspects of dealing with a publisher. Joanna Moriarty again, "Realistic expectations help—if the Publicity Department tells you, in the nicest possible way, that your book is unlikely to be featured on *Newsnight* it's best to believe them."

Taking in the full canvass of the area a relationship encompasses, she continues, "The author/publisher relationship works when there's a healthy respect for each other's expertise. Do remember that the publisher is making a substantial investment in your book, and they need it to pay off as much as you do. This means, for instance, that it's important that you trust their judgement about things like the cover. The Sales Director will have a huge amount of experience of making the most of the 90 seconds' attention they'll get for each title from key buyers, so they've chosen a particular design for a reason, even if you can't see how it does full justice to the content. A letter from all your neighbours and your milkman saying they prefer the illustration your daughter did—this is a real life example—just isn't going to help."

A joint enterprise

Additionally, and again speaking for many editors, Joanna turned to publicity. "Brazen self-promotion is very much appreciated. And, if this means displaying a certain degree of forthrightness in your dealings with the Publicity

Department, you will be forgiven provided you exploit your contacts just as boldly. Getting your book out there isn't something you can just leave up to the publisher nowadays—it's a joint enterprise. Do let people know what you're doing—a phone call late on Friday night to say 'I'm giving a talk in Colchester on Sunday, can you make sure some books are there?' will not help." She is right in every word she says. I must have worked with more than 20 editors over the years. All express similar thoughts; as Nikki Read, of *How to Books* put it to me bluntly, "Essentially publishing is about marketing."

A good editor can make or break a book. And a "good editor" is, in part, an editor working effectively with an author—the joint enterprise mentioned above. Creating the right relationship is largely down to you, it does not just happen, and aiming actively to create it is a good stepping stone on the road to making your authorship successful.

Beyond this, there are many ways in which elements of a book can promote an author and help sell more of their works. Here too collaboration between an author and a publisher is important, so let me mention a few pointers here too.

Making a book work promotionally

Few feelings beat that experienced by an author who sees their book on sale in a bookshop, especially if it is well displayed. But what is it doing? Just sitting there waiting to be bought? And what can it do to help you once it has been bought? Any book is potentially a promotional asset, and yet this aspect of its being does not just happen. What makes it act promotionally needs engineering and this is an area in which the author can exert some influence.

The first obvious element of the book that turns it from just so much paper into a working promotional device is the jacket. Fashions vary and covers can (will?) date (which is why long selling titles tend to be reissued from time to time in new jackets). What matters is that a cover looks good alongside other books and that it acts to inform, impress or intrigue in the vanishingly few seconds that someone may linger on it as they browse. Any sensible author will take an interest in the cover, though you need to remember that your taste is not the only factor. The only time I attempted to veto a cover on one of my books, I backed down when the publisher showed me three rough designs and said the one I disliked was the top choice of W H Smith!

For Non-UK Readers: W.H.Smith is a major British retailer who sell stationery and books across the U.K.

Cover apart, though, what other factors are there to consider? Well, several; amongst the main ones, some linked to the cover, are:

- *author's biography*: Here practice varies. Some books contain a fair amount of information about the author. With non-fiction, and if the expertise of the author is important to the credibility of a book, then details may influence sales. Other books say little or nothing. For instance, with *Jonathan Strange and Mr Norrell*, a first novel that received a lot of positive comment and where interest in the author, Susanna Clarke, was probably high, the paperback contained one line about her. Also there is the vexed question of an author photograph. You may feel that your face will help sales not at all, but you may also not be the best judge—and perhaps should be guided by the publisher. Certainly this area needs some thought and whatever does appear must be intended to help.
- *reviews*: These certainly help (provided they are good!) and will carry more weight if the reviewer is well known and respected. A paperback often carries a great many. First publication may present more difficulty, but persuading the right people to read a manuscript or proof copy can be worthwhile and is certainly something an author can do if the publisher will not take the time.
- *listing of other works*: many books do this, but unaccountably some do not and often this information appears as a stark list on a page otherwise blank. Why

not say something about each? A publisher may need more persuading to list other titles published by another publisher, but again the effort can be worthwhile.

Many other possibilities exist: a reference book may have a book mark in it carrying a promotional message, a Foreword might be written by someone whose name adds to the appeal of a book and, of course, many publishers have a website and encourage readers to use that as an electronic catalogue, one that often allows orders to be placed and from which readers can request a regular email newsletter about new publications. Another device that a website allows is special promotions: I recently saw a science fiction book offering, on its last page, a chance to "Win a trip to NASA". The reader could enter by requesting a catalogue or visiting their website. An increasing number of authors have personal websites and electronic newsletters and you see these featured in their book; sometimes an email address is there too allowing a personal response to be sent to any reader who makes contact. This is not just because the author wants to chat, though they may well value the feedback, it is also to allow them to sell.

More elaborate things are possible too. A book may end with a mention of a sequel, an additional or previous book by the same author. This may be a few words, a whole page—rather as the blurb for a book—and sometimes has a reproduction of the book's cover; this latter may even be in colour, as is done by printing on the inside cover of a paperback. The most elaborate version of this is the book that ends with some extract—perhaps the first chapter—of a new one. The intention is that the reader reads that and resolves to buy the new one. Alistair McCall Smith's books, which include *The No. 1 Ladies Detective Agency* series, feature both full colour jackets for other books on the inside cover and, on occasion, an advance chapter of his next book. His editor at the publishers, *Abacus*, Richard Beswick, told me that more of this sort of thing is being done—not just for well-known authors either—"sales potential is the prime consideration, and the author's view is important too" he said.

Just listing other titles costs little or nothing, but we are now into territory where costs become a real issue. Print in four colours on the inside of a paperback cover and the extra cost of production is significant. An author pushing for this may have to be more persuasive than with simpler suggestions, but it seems such opportunities *are* there.

So, when you are published, whether for the first or the umpteenth time, make sure you take an active role in all this, rather than simply accepting the publisher's first suggestion of how your book will appear. As ever, if you want to receive significant royalties, you need to take significant steps to encourage them.

The writers' army

A publisher has a big and complex job to do to get books into retail outlets; the storm troopers in this ongoing battle are the publishers' representatives, and as a further example of how collaboration with a publisher helps, let me mention them next.

Once your book is in print, and the excitement of seeing pristine copies on your shelf fading, you begin to wonder where all the other copies are. Are they prominently displayed in bookshops throughout the land, or languishing in some dusty warehouse?

You will have seen your title featured in your publisher's catalogues, but this is the tip of the iceberg. All sorts of promotional activity is probably going on and your particular title may be benefiting from some of this—a press release may be sent, review copies dispatched and so on. What will certainly happen is that as publishers' sales staff visit bookshops and other outlets (remember the wide range of outlets that sell books: from supermarkets to websites like *Amazon* and *The Good Book Guide*), they will be telling them about your book. A process, incidentally, called "subscribing" when a title is new.

This is a specialist and challenging job. More than 200,000 books are published in the U.K. every year. Your publisher may publish a large number of new ones every month, and have a backlist of many thousands of titles that need to be kept selling. The job must be done in a way that respects the trade; booksellers are busy and a representative will get only a limited time, often spent in some public area of a shop with distractions all around. Watch out for this happening, eavesdropping can be interesting! Such people have to deal with a wealth of matters: some good—negotiating increased display space—some not—arranging for the return of unsold books. The key factor that must be tackled, however, is time. There may be a good case to be made for a shop to stock a book but, except in rare cases, it will only command attention if it can be put over in one or two minutes. Not easy to do, and not easy to keep fresh.

So how can a writer help? First, assume you can. The sales director of a publisher of some of my books, rates the value of author assistance highly, especially in their own locality— "interpret 'local' widely" he says. Not least, he feels it makes the job more interesting to have contact with writers rather than simply selling the physical book. So what can you aim to do? A number of things:

First, write to the sales team—you will need to organise this through management—aiming to give them a list of interesting things to say in the course of describing your book to potential stockists. You might even be able to speak to them. Regular meetings of sales teams are held, when representatives from around the country get together; I have done this a number of times and it really puts you instantly into a different category from other authors they have not met.

Secondly, aim to contact—perhaps meet—whichever representative deals with your local area. Suggesting meeting them before they call on a local bookshop and offering a coffee break works well, "repping" can be a lonely job and the contact may be welcomed. During such a chat you may learn a great deal about a range of outlets: which ones it is worth you contacting, who to approach, what they have done in the past and found successful (so that you can make pertinent suggestions). You can also volunteer points that might usefully be made by the representative in their work; though in doing this, always remember the vanishingly small amount of time they will have for your particular title amongst all they have to do.

Keep in touch. They will not have time to meet you every five minutes, but may welcome another chat or look carefully at notes and ideas you send them in the post or by email. If you treat them as the experts, rather than trying to tell them how to do their job, such contact can be very productive—after all, any idea that helps sell more books is likely welcome.

There is a constructively symbiotic arrangement here. Both parties help the other. For example, if you discover that a local bookshop is planning a special promotion of a particular genre, and this fits your title, then coordinated approaches by both you and the representative may succeed in getting you prime space in a subsequent display. If sales are good, this is evidence for other propositions that either of you may make in future.

Many authors do not even know the name of their publisher's representative for their local area; much less liaise with them in any way. If this is you, put it right. To paraphrase a famous song: a little help from your friends is always welcome.

A good relationship with those who are effectively your customers, and this may imply numbers of people within a single organisation, is a sound foundation for much of your potential success. This area is well worth attention and what is said here gives a flavour of the task. What is said in this chapter links to ideas in Chapters 8 and 9 and, as those ideas show very clearly, there is much to do.

6 Telling the World

The quotation above is very apposite. Promotional activity can be expensive in terms of both time and money and, realistically the principle to pursue is one of doing a range of things sufficiently well to make a difference without letting the range of activities get out of hand. There has, after all, to be a balance and, not least, writing takes time too; lots of time you may well say. Any costs involved also need watching and any investment must ultimately pay for itself.

Promotional activity was touched on in Chapter 2 and many of the suggestions in Chapters 8 and 9 are concerned with promotion. Certainly there are many things to do ranging from events (book signings and readings, say, and also networking events such as conferences or meetings of writing bodies) to things like producing flyers, bookmarks, cards and more. It is not my purpose here to explore every possible technique in how-to detail, though I shall be pleased if there are matters touched on here you want to check out further. Here we consider a number of specific tasks, both to review how to go about them and demonstrate the overall principles involved whatever you may do.

Public relations

PR stands for both public relations, the overall activity of creating visibility and a positive image, and press relations in the media (anything from your local paper to a specialist journal in a field that's important to you). There is a good deal involved here, but the core issue in press relations is the press release and it is worth saying something about that. The first thing is to make sure that they get to the right people, check names and consider sending both a hard copy and an email version to key publications.

Composing a press release

There are two, perhaps conflicting, aspects of putting together a press release that will stand a good chance of publication. The first is to comply with the "form" demanded by the newspapers, magazines and journals to which you send your release; the second is to stand out as being of genuine interest from the very large number of releases received.

Consider the "form" first; this list covers most things, but every release does not need to follow every point slavishly:

- it should carry the words "Press (or News) Release" at the top, together with the date, preferably at the top left-hand side of the first page.
- if an embargo is necessary then it should be clearly stated: "EMBARGO: not to be published before (time) on (date)". You might use capitals for emphasis. (Note: an embargo is a request not to publish before a certain date, to ensure news items appear as near as possible together and do not pre-empt it. Once an item has been in print, others will consider it of less interest.)
- at the top you need a heading, not too long but long enough to indicate clearly the content of the release or to generate interest in it.
- space it out well with wide margins, reasonable gaps between paragraphs and so on. This allows sub-editors to make notes on it.
- if it runs to more than one page, make sure it says "continued" or similar at the foot of the page, even breaking a sentence at the end of the page will make it more likely people will turn over.
- similarly, to make it absolutely clear that there is no more, many put END at the foot of the last page.
- use newspaper style. Short paragraphs. Short sentences. Two short words rather than one long one.

- keep it brief, long enough to put over the message and on to a second page if necessary, but no more.
- the first sentences are crucial and need to summarise as far as possible the total message.
- avoid overt plugging (although that may well be what you are doing). Do not mention names etc. right at the beginning, for example, though write in a way that allows a lazy journalist to turn it into a news piece easily and quickly.
- try to stick to facts rather than opinions; views may be important, but facts should lead.
- opinions can be given, in quotes, and ascribed as such to an individual. This works well and can be linked to the attachment of a photograph (which should usually be a black and white print and clearly labelled in case it gets separated from the release).
- do not overdo the use of adjectives, which can jeopardise credibility.
- avoid underlining things in the text (this is used as an instruction in printing to put words underlined in italics).
- separate notes to the journal from the text as footnotes, for example, "photographers will be welcome"; or they could get printed as part of the story.
- never omit from a release, at the end, a clear indication of from whom further information can be sought and their contact details (even if this is on the heading of the first page).
- make sure finally that it is neat, well typed and presentable and that it lists enclosures or attachments. It may be obvious perhaps, but important.

So, how do you make your press release stand out? There are fewer rules here, but two points are certainly worth bearing in mind:

- do not "cry wolf". Save releases for when you really have a story. If you send a series of contrived releases, there is a danger that a good one among them will be ignored.

- make sure the story sounds interesting and, without overdoing things, be enthusiastic about it. If you are not, why would they be? Perhaps the only good thing in the world that is contagious is enthusiasm.

So public relations is an area that can produce not simply awareness of your activities, but also paint a particular picture of it—creating not only understanding, but a positive interest in your work that whets peoples' appetites for more information, prompts enquiries, re-establishes dormant contacts and reinforces your image with existing customers. You can use press releases more widely than just to the press. Doing just that, I include an example of a press release on the next page.

Press release

Don't read this book on public transport!

If you don't want to be reduced to a sniggering mess in public, read Patrick Forsyth's new book, *EMPTY WHEN HALF FULL—A Cantankerous Consumer's Compilation of Mistakes, Misprints and Misinformation* in the privacy of your own home. It can't fail to make you laugh out loud, with its incredible collection of gaffes, misprints and downright deviousness found in instructions, notices, marketing and advertising messages.

No area is exempt from Patrick's forensic eye for imprecise, incorrect or dishonest writing, from multinational companies and government bodies to prestigious publications. Examples from the book of the real life booboos range from the unfortunate: *"This manual has been carefully to remove any errors"*... to the idiotic *"Blackcurrant juice comes in two flavours—orange and strawberry"; "Scandinavian slippers—buy one get one free"*... to the infuriating: *"The Adobe Updater must update itself before it can check for updates. Would you like to update Adobe Updater now?"*... to the downright scary: *"Passengers must stay with their luggage at all times or they will be taken away and destroyed."*

Author of many business books and a specialist in communication skills, Patrick Forsyth knows a thing or two about writing. *Empty When Half Full* has been likened to Lynne Truss' international best seller, *Eats, Shoots and*

Leaves, in its humorous analysis of ungrammatical, poorly punctuated, sometimes surreal writing on labels, signs, instructions and advertising. But Forsyth's extensive business and marketing background enables him to comment on the serious aspect of poor communication and highlight genuine dangers to consumers.

"Some of the mistakes quoted have potentially serious repercussions," says Patrick. "But they are chosen primarily for their nonsensical quality and tendency to make us smile; perhaps we should rejoice that they made customers chuckle as they read the material from product providers produced with less care than we—or they—might wish."

"This is a must-read for all communicators," suggests David Horchover FCIM, author of *Sales Promotion.* "Great and avoidable gaffes in marketing and sales promotion are humorously exposed and lampooned by Forsyth's needle-sharp and witty observations."

Editors' Notes: *Empty When Half Full* is published by Bookshaker and available via Amazon at £9.99. For a review copy, email lucy@bookshaker.com. For further information, see www.patrickforsyth.com, and to arrange an interview with Patrick Forsyth, please call the author on 01621 859300 or email patrick@touchstonetc.freeserve.co.uk.

You're a star

In case some of the potential use of something like a press release seems somewhat beyond you, remember that as a writer you are a celebrity, at least in your own backyard. So how much publicity and sales can be created around your local area?

The number of places in which you would value seeing your book, or whatever, featured is doubtless daunting and the world is a big place. Often costs are prohibitive: a journey across the country will not be covered by the royalty on a dozen book sales. So starting near to home makes sense. Not only does this make things manageable, it also gives you an additional selling point—you are a local author.

First you need to make a plan:

- define the area that makes sense; a county perhaps in geographic terms—though do not omit a significant town just over the border.
- list the places/people you want to contact and how you will do it.
- prepare the approaches; for example, draft persuasive written approaches or think about a planned telephone call (and make some notes before you dial).
- consider the timing; when is the best time to take action (while a book is new gives you an edge, and bear in mind holidays, Christmas and other events—some you must avoid, others you can link your action to).
- make sure that you are not clashing in any way with your publisher and see if they can offer any support (even getting colour copies of the cover from them may help and may save money).
- make sure you have time to implement your ideas (you may have to set some priorities)… and then get going.

The opportunities

What should be on your list? The following examples are chosen to illustrate the range of things possible. First, bookshops: here you should liaise with your publisher or their local representative, but there is value in local initiatives. Bookshop buyers are busy but, if you can get a moment with them, you can offer to help, perhaps getting books displayed face out or linked to other promotional activity. If your book would link logically to some props for a window display, offer to loan them. A model airliner, borrowed from a travel agent, might sit next to your travel book and so on. Independent book shops may be more inclined to work with you in this kind of way than chains (where window displays may be centrally organised).

Local radio is perhaps one of the best of the promotional possibilities; BBC Essex, which is my local station, features books and authors on a regular basis. They also link to other stations, so once after being interviewed by them I soon got requests from several other BBC local stations and did telephone interviews with those further afield. This need not be daunting, but it's wise to think a little about how to do it in advance; for example, they will want a dialogue, so don't go on too long as you answer one question. Make sure bookshops have stock at the time you appear on the radio and they may like it if you mention them on air: "I know XYZ Books have it in their window." The same applies to commercial stations, community and even hospital radio.

Local newspapers and magazines may review your book, but are also interested in stories about local authors. Try creating a story. For example, Elizabeth Webb, who writes books for children about a witch (Madrigal), had her daughter dress up in a pointed hat and broomstick for a signing. It made for good photographs and the local newspaper gave it more space than might otherwise have been the case. Timed for Halloween this was well worth the effort and worked well.

Surely no one is better qualified to sell your book than you, so finding a basis for giving talks can give you platforms at which books can be signed, sold and create something too that the press might report. Many organisations want speakers; consider for instance U3A, Rotary and, where appropriate, special interest groups. Start to pursue opportunities well ahead. For example, a likely useful one for many authors is the Women's Institute. I am, dare I say, an officially approved WI speaker; but I needed to register to be auditioned, languish on a waiting list for a year, do the audition and, having done that, (and passed—phew!) found that they work way ahead. I subsequently have Branch meeting dates in my diary for more than a year ahead. If you are worried about speaking (and, some of the time, would surely be reading), check out what makes it easier; and again be prepared (see the next chapter). Link the nature of your book to the bodies approached. For example, Elizabeth Webb's books are ideal for children just beginning to read and she has successfully arranged events in schools to help both the reading process and her book sales (indeed she has also done this overseas, helping raise funds for disadvantaged children).

Maximising the effect

Finally, remember to link things together. When you have several things in train they draw strength from each other. Get on radio and tell shops about it in advance. Send local papers a press release and send them another one reporting what you did. If you prepare a talk about your writing, consider: might it also make an article you can place in something like a county magazine? Use copies of such articles to send to others... and so on.

The possibilities go well beyond this short section and this is certainly an area where, once started, one thought and one action can lead to another... and another. Once you have made a start, you might be surprised what direction it takes you in: today your immediate area—tomorrow the world!

Remember:

- locally you're a star.
- think positive.
- brainstorm ideas.
- make a plan.
- approach the process systematically.
- make your approaches persuasive.
- be persistent.
- get yourself prepared (even to the extent of developing new skills like public speaking).

All sorts of things are possible. Some, some writers rule out almost without thought as being impossible or difficult. One such, mentioned earlier, is going on radio; but maybe you should.

And after the traffic news...

One day perhaps you will get on "big" radio, BBC Radio 4 perhaps, but let's concentrate on something more likely. Local radio has a large, and loyal, audience. Some stations are primarily music led, others, certainly the BBC stations, present an eclectic mix of news and views. Operating throughout the day, they have a voracious appetite for material and a great deal of time to fill, so maybe—though competition is strong—they present an opportunity for you.

Do not reject them as too grand, all sorts of people appear on radio, and the advantages can be considerable. First, there is a direct impact on potential purchasers: your book is mentioned in some way and some listeners make a note and go out and buy a copy. Further, there are ancillary effects: you, and your publisher, can use the *fact—featured on BBC radio*—on other announcements, press releases and so on; it also provides back up evidence for your publisher's representatives to mention as they sell your title to bookshops. Looking ahead, because publishers like an author who contributes to publicity, and thus generates sales, it may even make it easier to obtain a contract for another book.

"Being on radio" can mean a number of things. Sometimes it is simply a mention or news item, but it can be an interview—and some of those can give the author significant time. For example, BBC Essex is a typical station (and my local one) and has various daily interview slots, sometimes for up to 30 minutes; allowing for other announcements, this can give the interviewee some 20 minutes of chat. Guests are not always writers, of course, but some certainly are, and some of those are invited more than once. This is not chance. In the case of BBC Essex who, like all such stations, researches its audiences carefully, it is deliberate policy. I spoke to Margaret Hyde, Managing Editor for the station, and she was clear: "We broadcast primarily to an audience from 50 to dead." She said, "They are interested in things local—like using local services including the library—they are volunteers, they have grown-up families; and we know they love books." So the station sees writers and books as a regular part of their content, "Especially," Margaret Hyde again, "when there is a people aspect to their story and when they, or their book, relate to something local." This may help a local history, or a book set in a specific region, but it may also just mean that the author lives locally. The station supports the Essex Literary Festival, an annual event, and presents a mix of items, from book reviews to interviews with authors and human-interest stories. They also like to give books away as competition prizes, so anyone aiming to be featured may want to persuade their publisher to make a few copies available.

Seeking an appearance

How do you organise to appear on local radio? Well, it may take some work, but it is possible. Margaret Hyde recommends more than one contact. She suggested first that, if the publisher sends a written announcement of some sort ("And send both an e-mail and hard copy," she said), then the author might follow up two or three times over a period of seven to ten days, writing or telephoning; or both. If what is sent is newsy, and it should be, then judge carefully when you send it: too far ahead and it may be put aside and become buried, even if it prompted initial interest. Too last minute and it may be rejected because schedules are full in the short-term.

While an approach that rings bells and is newsy in some way can prompt attention, regardless of the broadcasting experience of a writer, it makes sense for the writer to act appropriately. You should not make demands, you should respect the station's policy and practice and, just like editors, those involved in producing programmes are busy people— deal with them efficiently and they will like it. Any approach, whether by letter or press release, should be carefully written and aim to say something striking in a memorable way.

If, when, an invitation comes, turn up on time if you go to the studio (though you could be interviewed over the telephone) and respect the medium. For example, most radio items are short and interaction between interviewer and interviewee needs to be maintained. When the first question comes, resist the temptation to see it as an opportunity to pontificate at length—what works best is a number of short answers, rather than something that begins: *Well, I suppose there are three key messages in the book* and then attempt to fill ten or fifteen minutes uninterrupted. Speaking on radio is special and some study is recommended.

An invitation is a real opportunity to promote you and your book, and there is nothing quite like hearing the host say: *Our next guest is the writer...*

The internet and all that jazz

There are a host of ways to augment your publicity on line these days; indeed they change (and increase) as you watch, and this section risks dating almost immediately (which is why it does not detail what to do in how-to style). Much of the possible activity here is with so-called "inbound marketing": in simple terms, putting bread on the waters in a way that gets people contacting you ("found by customers" in the jargon).

Websites are now almost ubiquitous and many a writer has one, either to promote themselves and their work or actually to canvass orders for books; effectively dipping their toes in what is called e-commerce. Websites can be simple, and thus inexpensive (mine certainly is—www.patrickforsyth.com). Incidentally, logging on and checking out a few writers' websites may be useful research and help you form a view of what might suit you. But they can be useful, especially as so many people, once they are interested in anything, now instinctively go on line and check it out that way. If you have one, you need to keep it up to date, and also review its use, and if you do not then you may want to think about it.

Setting up a website

It is not my purpose here to explain the technology, indeed I am hardly qualified to do so. However, a website is no more than a new option in the promotional mix and needs to be considered accordingly. Setting up a website can be potentially time-consuming and expensive; so too can maintaining it and keeping it up to date. Some writers acted very early as technology created this opportunity. Though some acted solely because it was "something that had to be done", perhaps to keep up with others, perhaps to pander to their ego. Whatever the reason, it was sometimes ill-considered and time and money were spent to no good effect. Whatever might be done needs thinking through; the first question is very obvious and straightforward: What objectives do you have for your website?

There may be several, but they should all be specific. It is important to know whether the cost of setting this up is delivering what was intended; important, not least, to how the site is developed. Perhaps the site is in part a source of reference. You want people to consult it to obtain information (and be impressed by it at the same time). This may save time and effort otherwise expended in other ways. Perhaps you intend that it plays a more integral part in the selling process, and you want to measure its effectiveness in terms of counting the number of new contacts it produces and, in turn, how many of those are turned into actual revenue producing customers, so you need to keep records (and have a basis for counting how many people log onto it).

So, if you already have a website, check whether you have good feedback and if you are in the process of setting up a site—consideration of this is an inherent part of the process.

In addition, you may have products (books, talks etc.) you want people to order and pay for through direct contact with the site. Also you might offer something free, like a sample chapter to whet appetites. In this case, not only must the ordering system work well, and this means it must be quick and easy for whoever is doing the ordering, but the follow-up must be good too. Any initial good impression given will quickly evaporate if whatever is ordered takes forever to arrive or needs several chasers. One hazard to good service is to demand too much information as an order is placed. Of course, this kind of contact represents an opportunity to create a useful database; but turning ordering into the Spanish Inquisition will hardly endear you to (busy) people.

Whatever objectives are decided upon, there are then three distinct tasks. They are to:

- *attract people to the site*: just having the site set up does not mean people will log onto it in droves, much less that the people you want to do so will act in this way. Other aspects of promotion must draw attention to it and this may vary from simply having the website address on your letterhead and card to incorporating mention of it in talks or writing (as I have done here!).

- *impress people when they see it*: both with its content and its presentation. This means keeping a close eye on peoples' views and the practicalities as it is set up. For example, all sorts of impressive graphics and pictures are possible and can look creative and may well impress. Certainly you will need some. But such devices take a long time to download, and if that is what you are encouraging people to do they may find this tedious, especially if the graphics seem more like window dressing than something that enhances the content in a useful way.

- *encourage repeat use*: this may or may not be one of the objectives. If it is, then efforts have to be made to encourage re-contacting—regularly updating in a newsy fashion: a book going from hardback to paperback, a new cover, a good review and so on. This may involve an overlap with other forms of communication. Regular change makes this more likely to occur.

Beyond this, you also need to consider carefully:

- what the content should be (this is an ongoing job, not a one-off).
- how the contacting of the website can prompt a dialogue (a link to a blog, perhaps).
- how topical it should be (this affects how regularly it needs revision).
- its convenience and accessibility (does it have a suitable navigation mechanism?).
- will it look consistent (and not as if it has been put together by a committee).

- the protection it needs (is anything confidential, is it vulnerable to hackers etc.?).

Overall, it will need the same planning, coordination and careful execution as any other form of what is actually marketing communication. You may need to compare notes with friends and colleagues (though be careful not to overreact to one view).

In addition, someone needs to have the knowledge that is necessary from a technical standpoint; either you must bone up on this (and that can be done) or seek professional advice and assistance—though do not let an enthusiastic professional talk you into every bell and whistle as it can be expensive and unnecessary.

If a site is to be useful—that is an effective part of your "marketing mix"—then sufficient time and effort must be put in to get it right. And the ongoing job of maintaining it must be borne in mind from the beginning. For instance you may need to update events, replace pictures and add stop press news of your activities. Certainly there are no problems augmenting it. For instance, you might:

- make it mobile friendly (so that people can access you via mobile smart phones).
- add a blog (using something like Wordpress)—and, as a writer, yours should be better than most!
- use website optimisation techniques to get your site placed high when sites are searched for.
- include links to: publishers and booksellers (including Amazon), and events.
- add audio or video elements (perhaps via a link to YouTube).

This whole area changes and develops as you watch. For example another development is QR codes (it stands for quick response), a square shaped bar code like symbol that allows a smart phone user to log into a message they see on their phone. You increasingly see these on everything from advertisements to brochures or in shop windows (they are even on bus stops in Paris, zap one of those and you find out which bus to catch and when). So a book with a QR code on might allow a browser in a book shop to "tune in" as it were to an audio, video or text message to help them make a buying decision.

The usage of QR codes are comparatively new so who knows how it will all develop, but there are opportunities of this sort not to be missed but, as this short section makes clear, it needs to be approached in the right way or effort can be dissipated without real advantage.

Social media

Much is written about social media and their promotional power. Such include the likes of Facebook (this alone has over 800 million users), Twitter, Linked-In, the newer Google + and more; and it also includes a plethora of "chat rooms"—by which I mean more or less formal groups of like-minded people communicating regularly. *Writing Magazine* has one, and its users appear enthusiastic and content with what it does for them. So too do formal bodies of one sort and another; an example here is the Society of Women Writers and Journalists (this is an excellent and useful body of which I am a member—they have male members though we are in the minority).

It takes time to get into such things, to learn how they work and how they might be useful to you. It needs some initial research and, if you are interested, then it may be worth seeking out articles that brief readers on what to do and how it works. I will not try to describe the detail of every possible medium (not least because their features change almost as you watch). The key thing, in what is these days referred to as "viral marketing", is to initiate and maintain contact with people, especially those who are called "sneezers"; that is those people who are likely to pass on messages to others (preferably many others).

One caveat: writers are famous for what is called displacement activity—chores, tasks or rituals that for a moment *stop* you from writing. In the old days it was sharpening your pencils, now it is emailing, surfing the internet and attending to social media tasks. A good parallel here is committees. Being on a suitable committee can be useful, rewarding and fun; but being so is time-consuming. I am on two, no three, committees and that's about my limit. So I choose carefully what they will be. It is easy to get sucked into such things—a member resigns and you are petitioned to take over their place, for instance. Think first and pick wisely.

So it is too with social media. Maybe a blog would be useful, so too would be increasing your tweeting presence, spending more time on Facebook and... one could go on. The way forward is to consider the priorities (not just what's easiest) and the amount of time you can afford to invest in such things—that's time, let us be clear, when you will not be writing. Make conscious decisions and—vitally—aim to monitor the usefulness of what you do; doing any of this must prove time well spent.

There will doubtless be new distractions coming along, even before this book appears, check those too and apply the same criteria—there may be new things to do, but perhaps something must go to make room for them (remember your time is valuable).

The whole area of promotion is an important part of being sufficiently visible to make money from your writing. I am not advocating a massive campaign (unless you wish and have a story to tell that justifies), but there are a range of things to be done—some picked up amongst the range of ideas set out in Chapters 8 and 9.

7 Stand-up comic

The human brain starts working the moment you are born and never stops until you stand up to speak in public.
Sir George Jessel

An acquaintance of mine worked for some six years part-time as a groundsman for a college, mowing the playing fields and suchlike, to allow time to write—while his wife commuted to London and held down a good full-time job to keep them solvent. Eventually he was rewarded by a three book deal and a dozen books later he, top science fiction writer, Neal Asher, is very successful and divides his time between England and Crete. He does everything a successful novelist should, but he is not keen on public speaking and so limits what he might do in this particular area. He is not alone.

Most people feel some unease about any sort of formal presentation. Maybe it is best not to talk of nerves. Better maybe to call it creative apprehension, as did one literary festival speaker asked just before the kick-off if he was nervous (*If you're not nervous, why are you in the "Ladies"?*). But delivering a speech can be worrying—after all, there may be a great deal hanging on it.

Some avoid it. Even amongst those who do it, some persist in winging it. They seem to think that a moment's thought will suffice. Or they do prepare, but they do so unthinkingly, on automatic pilot; like those that look fixedly over their shoulder at a screen and away from their audience as they read verbatim what it says on a slide.

Furthermore, I regularly hear the excuse given for a lacklustre performance—*there was not enough time to prepare*. Yet the alternative to preparation is not just a poor—perhaps embarrassing—performance, it is failing to achieve objectives; and maybe wasting time and money and leaving much to do to retrieve the situation (if that is possible).

Mind you, you need an audience and even at something simple like a signing this is sometimes a problem. "I ended up buying them a cup of coffee and giving them a copy of the book". The speaker is Chris Stewart, author of a series of books starting with *Driving over lemons*: he was describing the first time he spoke at a bookshop and only two people turned up. Such can be a daunting experience, though Chris's success now pulls in a good audience and he is a droll and entertaining speaker.

The nightmare

We all have to do lots of things we do not like. Some are just distasteful things like unblocking the sink or cleaning someone else's ring off the bath, others are worse—things we feel seriously ill-equipped to do well. And take speaking: we can all have a chat, swap gossip or say, "*What time do you call this?*" to the postman, but sometimes we may have to do something rather more formal. But ask many writers to stand up and address an audience and they go to pieces, or to Reykjavik. Anything at all rather than do it—it seems that even writers, who have a way with words, can feel inadequate.

Be warned: stand up totally unprepared and, oh dear, things can go wrong. People stumble, they hesitate, and they sweat. They begin every other sentence with the superfluous word "*Basically*". They say "*Um, err... at this moment in time perhaps I could read you a sort of piece, well an extract really, it's not too long and...*" Such can sound unprofessional and apologetic, when they should be establishing real rapport.

Just when they should impress their audience, exude confidence and use words as effectively as they do on the page, they upset or confuse them. Exactly what is said and how it is put matters. As Bob Hope used to say of his early performances, "*If the audience liked you, they didn't applaud, they let you live.*"

At worst, people go on too long, their explanation explains nothing and where they are going is wholly unclear. Some fidget endlessly, others remain stock still gripping the table or lectern in front of them until their knuckles go white and fear rises from them like a mist. Still others are apt to pick holes in people in the audience, or their noses. If they use slides, then they can only be read from the back of the room with a telescope, a fact made worse by their asking brightly, "*Can you see all right at the back?*" despite the fact that there is precious little they can do about it if the answer is "*no*", and in any case they should not be asking, they should *know* their slides are legible. They barely pause for breath, as they rush from one word to the next, many of them inappropriately chosen and as many more too long. Indeed, the only long word of which some writers appear ignorant is rehearsal.

Of course, a lucky few believe that making a speech or presentation is second nature. They know they can wing it. They are convinced that they know their stuff and how to put it over. The first rule then for the inappropriately overconfident is, of course, to assume that the audience is as thick as they look and will, provided the right level of impenetrable gobbledegook is hit, instantly conclude that they are in the presence of a master.

They take "winging it" to mean that if they want people to actually understand even the gist of what is said, then some care must be taken. So, they talk v-e-r-y... s-l-o-w-l-y; use simple words, and generally proceed on the basis that the audience members have the brains of a retarded dormouse. They spell out complicated bits in CAPITAL LETTERS, speaking **more loudly** as they do so. Though they are always careful not to be condescending, as that will upset people (you *do know* what condescending *means* don't you?).

For this kind of speaker, being on their feet is something to savour. They need only the briefest of introductions and they are away, moving quickly past the first slide without noticing that it is upside down, the coins in their trouser pocket rattling at 90 decibels (well, the men) and the audience hanging on their every repetitive mannerism as they mutter to themselves, "*If they scratch their ear whilst stood on one leg again, I'm walking out".* It makes lesser mortals feel all too sadly inadequate—even the famous: it was Mark Twain who reportedly said, *"It normally takes me three weeks to prepare a good impromptu speech."* Poor man; just as well he was a good writer.

Standing up in front of an important audience knowing that they would rather chew off their own fingers than sit and listen to someone who cannot make the simplest point clear, is rather like being pushed into a lion's den. Without an understanding of how to go about it in the right way, you will be in deep, deep trouble. No audience will warm to a writer who is ill-prepared and who flounders through a speech that is tedious, confusing and poorly delivered; nor are they likely to buy from them. And nor will they either if the speaker is poor through unthinkingly believing they can wing it. Furthermore, no poor speaker is likely to magically acquire the requisite skills instantaneously in the few seconds between being introduced and rising to their feet to speak.

So, if you are not in fact a natural, and few people are, you need to give it some thought before you get to your feet. Once you are actually in the lion's den it is a little late to discover that salvation is not guaranteed by saying, *"Nice pussycat."*

Getting it right

Okay, nightmare over. There is a real opportunity here, it may be one that demands some preparation, but for many a writer who learns to do it well, it can pay dividends. The first rule about presentations is to prepare: always and adequately.

Two immediate dangers of lack of preparation are:

- *reading*: unfamiliarity with the material may make it seem easiest to read something verbatim. Never do this. It is one thing to read extracts of your writing (though it's worth practising, printing out pages in a good-sized type and thinking about how you do this—a clipboard suits me), it is another to read the "speech" portion of what you say. Do that less than perfectly and it says clearly to the audience—*I did not have time to prepare*, or worse, *I'm nervous*. You need to prepare clear notes, but to speak *from*, not read. Much of them may be just headings and small prompts to what and how to proceed.

- *over-dependence on slides*: this has become known as "death by PowerPoint" and is again often a direct result of lack of preparation. Never put too much information on one slide, pick a suitable typeface and never say— *can you see this at the back?* You should know they are visible. Ditto audibility. There is a famous response to the question, "Can you hear me at the back?"; the reply, "Yes, but I'm prepared to swap places with someone who can't!" Sorry, I digress. It is wisely said that slides need not make complete sense until you say something and begin to make the points they flag. If a slide says it all, what is the role of the speaker? Slides are not always necessary or appropriate of course, but when they are they must be well used and must support not lead.

It can be done however. Any author can make an acceptable, workmanlike presentation and many find that it is something at which they can excel if they go about it correctly. Few people are natural presenters (I know!); those that make it look easy tend to do so because they work at it. Most people feel some unease about it. At worst, people go on too long, and where they are going is wholly unclear. Some compound the problem with mannerisms, a clear lack of confidence or slides that appear upside down. Why? Nerves overtake them.

Beating your nerves

So how do you calm your nerves, and take advantage of what has been described as an "open goal", an opportunity to impress, entertain and sell yourself and your work?

The first rule is to think positive, because fear can mean that most thoughts can be negative—*I can't do it, they won't like it, what do I say?* Consider the audience. They actually *want* it to go well. What else? Audiences respond to a good presenter, especially one that focuses on and respects *them*. Indeed people may be secretly grateful that *they* are not the ones speaking.

List all your fears, and take practical steps to deal with the causes one by one. For example, if you worry about:

- timing: *rehearse, time it and make sure your notes include a guide on timing.*
- losing your place: *again, the style of your notes should make this unlikely.*
- dry mouth: *always have a glass of water to hand, no one minds if you take sip.*
- what to do with your hands: *hold something—something appropriate like a pen.*
- visual aids: *can they be seen? Check ahead of your talk, then you know (and never say "Can you see at the back?"—people expect you to know all is well).*
- pausing: *count to yourself to ensure you do not rush on when you need a dramatic pause.*

Be prepared

That said, what makes it work? Preparation is vital; yes, it's important enough to repeat. It ensures something worthwhile is delivered to the audience, and *knowing you are prepared is the greatest boost to confidence that you can get.*

First, think about *what* you need to say, and what you should *not* say.

Comprehensiveness is never an option and often time pressure makes encapsulation essential. Think about the order in which you will say things; and where you will fit in anything you read. Make sure it is in a logical sequence and plan to explain your choice. You will need to get off to a good start, so the first few moments need especial thought—they make your audience want to hear more, and give you confidence: *It's going well.* Limit the number of main points, and make each one a mini-presentation with its own beginning, middle and end and with a manageable number of subsidiary points under each topic. Allow time to exemplify and illustrate as well as to describe. Effectively, give yourself a clear agenda from which to work.

How to say it

Only after you have a clear plan, give thought to *how* you will put things over. Trying to create a talk, thinking simultaneously of *what* to say and *how* to say it is certainly complicated. Think particularly of how you can achieve:

- *clarity*: never underestimate either the difficulty of achieving clarity, or the impressiveness that comes when something is explained easily and clearly. How often do I hear people saying things like—*well, I suppose it is basically sort of…*—not what they would ever write and what exactly does it *mean*? You surely *know* what makes your writing special, take time to work out a way of making others clear about it too.
- *description*: similarly make sure that you are genuinely descriptive. Saying something is *sort of slippery* is descriptive but imprecise; saying it is *as slippery as a freshly buttered ice-rink* not only says more, it is much more likely to be remembered.

Make *notes* from which to speak (and slot pieces of your work to be read within them). Set out the main points, add a note of subsidiary ones, note key things in full perhaps, and go over it until you are sufficiently familiar with it to speak from that. Mark the emphasis; use symbols—!—or write, *Pause*. Time it. Allocated half an hour or whatever, it gives great confidence to stand up *knowing* that it will take the right amount of time.

Getting the details right

There is more, of course. You may want to use slides (not too much information on each); if so, make sure that you are familiar with the equipment and that it works. Having everything organised, *knowing* that you can read your notes, will finish on time, can project your voice—just talk to the furthest person from you—and not trip over the wire to the projector, all help quell nerves. Being able to maximise the opportunity may demand some study and certainly some preparation; but the effort is worthwhile.

Sometimes you need a lighter touch. Be careful. It can work well, but the moment you say something like, *Here's a funny thing*, it had better be funny. Quips, quotes and anecdotes can, however, work well, especially if they fit neatly with what you are saying and enhance your message rather than just being an aside. Dare I risk an example? Okay: when talking about the sheer power of English to express meaning I sometimes quote Isaac Asimov (who wrote nearly 500 books in his career). At some point it is said that someone asked him what he would do if he was told he only had six months to live. He thought for a moment and answered in just two words, *Type faster*. That usually brings a smile; but it also says such a huge amount.

Knowing the environment

You must know, or organise if possible, the speaking environment. As well as knowing the equipment, work out where to stand to allow the group to see the screen and you to see your notes. Make sure you have sufficient space available for your papers, tape the projector lead to the floor so that you do not trip, count the steps to the podium—and more…whatever the environment, reduce fears by being familiar with it.

Over time, analysing your talks after you have made them and planning changes—more of this, less of that—gives you more certainty of the next one being easier and going better; and also reduces any fears that it will not.

Reaping the rewards

The rewards of developing public speaking skills are considerable. What is more, good habits, factors that help make things go well like speaking at an appropriate pace and volume, do set in, a process that is more likely to occur if you set out to make it so. If you develop the habit of preparing, for example, and develop good habits regarding exactly how you go about it, then you will find your whole approach will act to help the end result. A good system for preparing your notes will prompt you to ask yourself if there should be a visual aid at certain points, and whether there are sufficient of them overall, and to do this more certainly and effectively. Good and sufficient visual aids will, in turn, augment what you say. The thinking and the process create a positive loop. Moreover, practice will soon begin to take some of the chore out of the whole process. Preparation does not take so long for those who have learnt how to go about it and who have a good system for doing it. Even seemingly awkward factors, such as judging how long a message will take to run through, become more certain with experience.

An added something

Beyond all this, to a degree, the sky is the limit. The best speakers make it look very easy, though this may simply disguise careful preparation, rehearsal and execution. Training, study (another plug: my book, *How to craft successful business presentations and effective public speaking* [Foulsham]), practice and sensible consideration of how you have done can help everyone move towards an acceptable standard. But it can do more than this. Charisma, often regarded (indeed defined) as a gift, actually consists (certainly in part) of intentionally applied techniques. Good eye contact, appropriate verbal emphasis, a careful choice of words and gestures, the confidence to hold a pause—and more—cumulatively add to the charisma-rating someone may be regarded as projecting. But such techniques can all be learned, developed and deployed to enhance the overall effect. This is not to say that such a process is contrived. Something like genuine enthusiasm is infectious. For the rest, in many ways it adds up to a respect for the audience and the occasion. The last thing people want is to sit through a lacklustre event. Any writer who works at how they do it, uses the available techniques appropriately and lets their personality contribute, will make the best job of it, helping both the audience and themselves. The alternative, a dreary talk and an audience who resent it, is not a happy one.

If you have already had some practice, considering what you are doing against the knowledge of the principles set out here (and more) will help you seek to achieve an even higher standard. If you are nervously awaiting your first outing: think about it and remember the old adage: *The golden rule for all presenters is to imagine that you are in the audience—* but do go for it. Aim to surprise yourself, and your audience. Who knows, you may just find that it is fun!

With some thought and good preparation you can make a real impression, one that will swell sales; see the summary below to add some confidence. Take a sip of water, a few deep breaths, and off you go—*Ladies and Gentlemen...*

Key points to boost confidence:

- always prepare thoroughly.
- list fears, think through what causes them and seek solutions.
- think positive (remember you are actively dealing with fears).
- focus on what to say (and read) and how to say it.
- understand the techniques you can use.
- check and organise the speaking environment.
- analyse your talks and make changes to ensure you learn from experience.
- remember the audience want it to go well.
- overall, regard it as an opportunity (a good presentational style can achieve so much).
- and... motivate yourself by thinking about how it can help sales!

8 Systematic action—a wealth of ideas

As has been said, you need both to resolve to take regular, considered and effective action on an ongoing basis to promote your work and to create a situation from which you can see financial success flowing. The difference between success and failure—getting something published and a subsequent cheque—may be minor: one small difference in what you do or how you do it may take you over the edge and have a manuscript you put in front of an editor being accepted.

The whole purpose behind the regular "Going to market" column I write for *Writing Magazine* is to point up ideas that might make this difference. It is intended to emphasise the need for a series of ideas, to suggest some (or remind people of some of the things they know but may sometimes neglect) and make turning such things into action just a little easier.

Over a few years, these columns have comprised an eclectic mix of thoughts and ideas; again this is the intention. And in adapting some and reproducing them here, the intentions are similar. They are intentionally in no significant order, nor do they attempt to be a comprehensive list of what to do. But I believe all make a good point—so this is perhaps a section of the book to be dipped into rather than read at a sitting. It is one, too, which you may find it useful to make notes about. If you find an idea you should or might use, do note it, keep the note and use it to prompt the idea into your own work or adapt it so that it suits—such ideas are valuable even if they can't be used as is and need some adaptation. There are sufficient thoughts here to create two chapters and I find it difficult to imagine that any reader will not find some ideas that they can use.

The very form of these two chapters makes an immediate point; it is good if you can succeed in getting paid twice (or more!)—as I am doing here—for the same thing, even if a little adaptation is necessary to make this possible. In this case, the twice is first in a magazine and then in a book (though such could happen the other way round). But it could be multiplied in a variety of ways, depending on the extent of the amendment: in the U.K. and overseas, in different types of magazine, even in more than one book— many combinations are possible.

That said, let's move on to the ideas: first, one that commends a dose of realism.

Be realistic

Some (many?) writers have an odd and illogical attitude to their work, or rather to the process of obtaining commissions. Consider your morning post. Today mine arrived as I started to write this (around 2 pm, but I digress!). It contained, amongst other things, a letter from a local furniture store announcing their annual sale, information claiming to be the best deal in credit cards imaginable and details of a local accountancy practice suggesting that their undertaking my accounts and tax work would save me large, but unspecified, amounts of tax—a fairly typical crop of such approaches.

Now, make no mistake, I do occasionally respond to direct approaches; sometimes people or organisations who write or telephone—and these days email too—make a good case, one corresponding with something I happen to be interested in and business is done to the satisfaction of both parties. So, while some such approaches are a nuisance, I would not want to receive none at all.

In this particular case, none seemed either relevant or irresistibly put. And so, and just dwell on this, *I do not intend to reply to any of them.* In so doing, or not doing if you prefer, I shall have not a jot of regret, embarrassment or contrition. I do not particularly feel for them, it is their problem if their targeting or approach is inaccurate; anyway, I am sure that they receive a sufficient rate of response to pay their way.

Fact: essentially this is no different to the writer sending an idea or manuscript to an editor. Sometimes your approaches will fall on stony ground, prove inappropriate, albeit only at the moment they arrive, and will be ignored. The response is not to be upset or feel slighted. It is the way the world is.

Deal with it. Persevere and send out some more.

With a little help from your friends

If you attend a writers' group, it doubtless meets regularly and such sessions can be both enjoyable and useful. It can be just a bit of fun, writing something the chairperson's theme for the session prompts, or—let's be honest—fitting something you want to write anyway to the theme. But such groups can also provide a trial run: an opportunity to read out loud almost always throws up something you want to change. Something may read a little awkwardly and a few words changed improve it, or it may be that, as you read, a whole better way of dealing with something pops into your mind. If you want it published, then it is perhaps a step nearer to getting into print.

Topics for such groups are decided in various ways. Members may contribute ideas or the chair may aim to have a wide range of topics and may also specify the form of the writing: fiction, non-fiction, poetry or whatever. But sometimes the link with publication can be more direct. The topic may be simply to write something for such-and-such a magazine, for instance. Then the task before the next meeting must involve some research: what is the magazine like? What topics might suit it? How long and in what form should it be? The resultant pieces may well be worth submitting, either immediately or after some revision.

If you want to be published, then using a writing group as a specific part of your quest can certainly be useful. Of course, some assignments can be nothing but fun. But addressing this issue formally is worthwhile; maybe a set proportion of sessions should be aimed specifically towards achieving publication.

Invest in success

Speaking at a writers' group, someone bemoaned to me about spending more than ten pounds sending a manuscript to an agent. Seemed a pretty good deal to me, the agent had seen two chapters and *wanted* to see the rest; some people never get such a wonderful opportunity to spend ten pounds. But, okay, postage *is* expensive.

Think about it though, if you are to get published and make money from it, then there are certain things you have to do and do right. Any cost of so doing is the price of entry, as it were, and postage is but one element of it. Expensive? Certainly. Worthwhile? You must judge, but one thing is for sure: you can only maximise your chances by taking such action on the basis of what is right for *the recipient*. Personal preference, your convenience and to some extent cost are not part of the judgement.

My "Going to market" column is delivered by email (the publisher's choice) and it is easy for both of us. The finished manuscript of many a book is delivered the same way. When contracted and expected, it will arrive in the form needed to edit and produce the finished book from it. But can you expect someone to print out—using their time and money— something you are hoping to interest them in publishing? No, you cannot. If it needs posting, so be it. Pack it, take it to the post office and regard the cost as an investment.

Email needs some consideration too. It may be easiest for you, but often a letter enclosing whatever needs to go with it may be better. Most people prefer their dinner guests to thank them with a card or letter rather than with an email. So too with publishers: communicate with them in the way *they* think best.

Odd odds

Writing groups are great gripe forums, but a comment at one I attended recently set me thinking. Entry details for a competition were passed round prompting one member to state, *No, thank you—£18 to enter; you would have to be very confident to do that.* No one contradicted, it seemed tacitly agreed that the thought was outrageous; surely no one would shell out that amount of money speculatively?

Well, would they? As they say about the National Lottery— *You have to be in it to win it.* Thus, by definition, the winner of the £18 competition *will* have spent that amount up front. What is more, if there are significant numbers of people who resent paying out money in this way, then being one who does so is surely giving yourself better odds.

Writing, at least writing to earn some money, does require that you embrace the old adage about speculating to accumulate. Even if you rationalise that you would have the computer anyway, you still need to buy paper, postage stamps, and telephone time; and the costs of researching what you write may be much more. If you regard your writing as a business, albeit a little one, then some costs must simply be taken as given. What matters is the difference between expenses and income. To have a negative emotional response to certain costs (and, yes, the competition organisers may well be aiming to make a profit), acts only to reduce the number of publications in which you can try to place your work. Make considered—businesslike—decisions by all means, but be realistic, accommodate some costs and cast your net wide.

Or maybe the National Lottery is better; millions of people seem unfazed by odds of fourteen billion to one, or whatever it is. Just write: 6, 23…

Check, CHECK

More from the writers' group gripe department: *Another rejection, not only have they turned me down, but they picked up some typographical and spelling errors too.* Of course it is depressing to get anything rejected, and often for no clear, or stated, reason. But of one thing you can be sure: if a manuscript is not carefully checked and contains errors then this will surely not help.

Think of the signals it sends out. A busy, pernickety editor starts reading and is interested, but once they see an error (particularly something obvious) their expectations immediately decline. Instead of saying, *This seems good, let's read on,* they say, *Oh dear, another slapdash effort.*

Of course checking can be a chore; and you doubtless need to do it more than once. It is difficult too. Spellcheckers leave things for you to spot (the likes of *no* and *not*; where a missing letter leaves a wrong word, the checker approves), and furthermore you simply get very close to things—you read what you are convinced you wrote, rather than what is actually on the page.

So care is necessary. And there are tricks: for example, on short pieces, people commend reading the text backwards; certainly when you are unable to rush on and have to look at it word by word, that helps pick up certain mistakes. Another way is to swap the final checking with a friend: they read your manuscript and you read theirs. If you swap with someone, there is an element of fairness about the time it takes—and it is amazing what a new pair of eyes can spott (sic). You both benefit.

Accuracy matters, (certainly you do not want the editor to leave a nought off your cheque!) and it can increase your rate of acceptance. Oh—thanks for reading this over, Sue.

Profitable filing

In the world of offices, it is said that less than ten per cent of the papers filed are ever looked at again; ruthlessness is necessary or organisations would literally disappear under the piles. But writers should consider what they keep very differently and with an eye on future profit.

Sometimes we realise that a piece of writing has no merit and deserves to go in the waste bin. But an essentially good article, say, written speculatively and turned down by several magazines may be tossed away in disgust and no record kept of it. But reworked later, it might be turned into something that is instantly accepted. It might result in a fee not only that might not have been received otherwise, but which is also achieved without great work, as the final article was half-written anyway. Reworking may take many forms. Maybe it is just that a longer or shorter version of something can be made viable. Maybe a new theme is superimposed on an original idea, making it suitable for publication at Christmas time or in a way that links to an event or anniversary. Maybe the end can be the beginning or the beginning the end; it does not matter as long as it is looked at with an open mind and a new possibility is found.

So only press the delete button after careful consideration. Arrange some designated "parking places", and keep them organised. File things by topic or likely market rather than lumping everything together under "Pending", which soon becomes unmanageable. I even have one file labelled "Maybe"! Review the contents regularly. Ideas or events can trigger you to revisit something perhaps months or even years old, and find that today the basic idea can be turned into something useable. For some people this is a regular source of market success.

Make it new

It is said that the most powerful word in marketing is to tell customers that something is "new". For example, in the fashion world, clothes seen in many retailers change every couple of weeks. Wise shopkeepers change their displays and shop windows (or some element of them) regularly; very regularly. And *Readers' Digest* uses the word "new" four times in every letter they mail.

Sometimes other matters interfere with the principle. Because of contractual arrangements in the film industry, the covers of DVD boxes are usually reduced versions of film posters, an approach that does not always promote clarity, as half the content can be illegible. But books do better. For example, if a book is published in hardback, then the paperback will usually appear with a different cover to give it a new look. So too with things you use to promote yourself. A letter, brochure or fact sheet is not a puppy; it's not for life. It needs regular updating and change if it is going to be relied on to strike the next person you send it to as new. More so if you are re-contacting people, perhaps those who have commissioned you previously. Approach letters are like curricula vitae (CVs)/resumes; there is no such thing as a standard one. However useful—and easy—it is to hold "standard" documentation on your computer, to make it as effective as possible it may well need some change each time you use it.

The moral is clear: keep everything you send out fresh, make it new, label it new too if appropriate and remember that its very newness contributes to making it work for you.

Profitable networking

Writing is always said, with some truth, to be a lonely business. Few writers' time is spent in a whirl of publishers' lunches, signing sessions and readings, even the most successful spend many hours with noses to grindstones, and you only have to read a single issue of a writing magazine to know that discipline is the order of the day.

In many ways, though, maybe writers should get out more. One human contact that is always useful is networking with other writers. Writers' groups can be an element of this, though here I mean specific liaison with individuals. For example, I visited the London Book Fair and did so with another writer. We did not follow each other round slavishly, but met up periodically to compare notes, rest our legs and have a drink. En route to a mid-afternoon cuppa, my colleague persuaded me to visit one additional stand. Publishers are busy at such events and most of their time is spent with buyers not authors; nevertheless we exchanged a few words with an editor and managed to arrange a meeting after the Fair. Time well spent: I ultimately obtained a contract and a book was published in due course (followed actually by a second). Yet it was not my initiative that led to this and, but for the fact that two of us had gone together, it would not have happened.

This is one example from a number of regular networking contacts with whom I liaise. The process is fun, interesting, stimulating and—above all—it leads to things happening that would not happen otherwise. Everything from a word on the telephone to an exchange of emails may help, and meetings and outings add to the possibilities. Try it.

Keeping at it

Every writer needs to put some bread on the waters. Well targeted and well executed approaches to new contacts can produce a response or a direct commission and, if well managed over time, can lead to a long-term relationship. This might prompt a number of articles over a few months or longer, or several books over some years.

There are all sorts of imponderables here. You have to make time for things: both finding new contacts and preparing and sending appropriate approaches. You have to have suitable ideas and make appropriate suggestions and you may have to be persistent: if the first contact produces nothing, then you may sensibly re-contact again, maybe several times. Generally speaking, the more initiatives you put in train the more responses you will get, providing the quality of what you send out is maintained. But writers can be arch procrastinators. You look at what might be an opportunity, highlighting a news item in *Writers' News* perhaps (see page 20), then rationalise the opportunity away. *It's not quite right; I need a better idea*; or simply, *I'll do it later* are the kind of thoughts that buzz around. Delay too long and the moment passes—*It's too late now.*

Most of us have a kind of threshold: some things are clearly opportunities and we rush to make contact. Others leave us uncertain. As we think about them, we seem to produce more reasons *not* to follow them up than to do so. So, simply a resolve to be more "bullish" can easily "beef up" the number of approaches made (if you'll pardon the pun)—and acceptances achieved. It will probably increase the number of rejections, or simply non-replies, as well but, hey, we need to think of that as par for the course. Being more positive, going for it a little more often, may be all you need to boost success.

The ghost of a chance

I have been ghost writing a non-fiction book recently (my name may not get on the cover, but some of the money will go into my bank account!). Part of my role was not just to organise the content and get the words down on paper, but also to find a publisher and lead the ongoing communications with them, indeed the split of monies reflects this role as well as that of writing.

Despite my thinking of it as an attractive title for a specialist publisher, initially more than one of the publishers I approached declined politely. Then an acceptance arrived. It was a good publisher and an ideal match with the title, but they wanted the "author" to guarantee to buy some copies to help them ensure that the venture would be profitable. Agreement to do this secured the contract, which was drawn up to include this arrangement and specified purchase terms allowing a profit to be made from selling on the books bought. This is a financial benefit to the publisher, and helps when they decide on the appropriate first print run. It also has psychological impact: indicating a belief in, and commitment to, supporting the author's title that strengthens confidence in the project. This is in no way a vanity deal; the publisher is mainstream and will support and sell the title in all their usual ways. Such a deal may be worth considering or suggesting, and might even be a factor in turning a potential no into a yes.

Here the confidence has paid off for all concerned. Systematic promotion and has led to the initial quantity purchased by the author being sold ahead of publication (to clients of the business the author runs); one company has ordered more than 200 copies, and the initial guaranteed quantity will be increased, with all concerned making more money.

Achieving sales appeal

Some things take longer than others. I have just received a contract for something I have been very keen to write after three years of attempting to sell the idea. Like me, you may console yourself in such circumstances that what matters is your current workload; it matters less if some of what you have confirmed has had a long gestation period and, realistically, this may vary. Some things are confirmed in the blink of an eye, others take time—sometimes a long time. So be it.

When you send things out, the question most people ask themselves is, "Will someone think it is publishable?" For many people, this is interpreted as meaning, "Is it a good piece of writing?". Some of the answer to that can be found in questions like: is it well written? Is the grammar correct? Are its sentences of reasonable length and does that length vary a bit? And, confident about your writing, you may feel positive about the answer to all such questions. But what should be asked is really a little different: "Will someone see it as *saleable*?" "Will someone believe people will pay money for it?" Material tends not to get published for its inherent quality, more for its commercial possibilities. This is true for a book and so it is too for an article—an editor wants articles that will assist the sale of their magazine.

Sometimes you will get rejections and, on occasion, suggestions as well. If so, remember that any changes you may be aimed towards, and any revisions you may make as a result, should not only be designed to fine-tune the writing (few of us are perfect and this may surely be necessary), they should also be aimed at better fitting your writing to its market. Make it saleable, and you are more likely to sell it.

Long-term contact

I once had a book proposal agreed within 24 hours of it being sent. Great, but note the "once"! Conversely, I once persistently maintained contact for three years with an editor after they moved to a new company—then received the largest single commission (in words and money) I have ever had. I congratulated myself on not giving up, but I thought about it too. I had only had six contacts over those three years, all consisted of my sending something, then telephoning. One call resulted in a meeting—tea in (the late lamented) *Borders* in London's Oxford Street—but no immediate commission. When the work did come, however, they contacted me; I was still high on their list of "useable authors" and, when finally they had something that fitted, they got in touch. The time the ongoing contact had taken was not large; indeed in relation to the work resulting, to say it was cost-effective would be an understatement.

The moral here is clear. Do not give up too soon. It helps if you keep a clear contact record. It only necessitates a few notes, but record a blow-by-blow account of what you—and your contacts—do: every letter, email and telephone call and every meeting too. Then you can judge when it is time to make contact again and keep the process going as long as you wish. Ring the changes too, an email last time, a letter next (people do not have to print a letter out and it may more likely be kept). And always say something more interesting to them than pleading, *more work please.*

Since the books mentioned earlier were commissioned and completed: nothing. The guy has again moved companies, but as a result of networking, he did buy me an excellent dinner; I shall certainly keep in touch—and we will see.

Well presented

It is all too easy to write something that does not quite do the job intended. For some people, the evidence of this is very public. For instance, for a while those staying in a Northamptonshire hotel would have seen a sign on the inside of their bedroom door that said: *In the interest of security, please ensure that your bedroom door is fully closed when entering or leaving your room.* A good trick if you can do it. Someone wrote this, got it printed and fixed to every guest room in the hotel and *still* no one noticed it was nonsense. (Incidentally, it was seeing this that got me collecting such things and ultimately resulted in the publication of *Empty when half full*, mentioned on page 61).

A mistake of this nature in a letter to an editor, a proposal or synopsis will do you no good at all. Care is needed in writing, checking must never be skimped and what is read must be what you meant. Maybe such communications should also include magic phrases that increase the chances of a positive response. But do such phrases exist? Well, people seem to believe that they do. Publishers report that submissions are much more inclined to use introspective phrases such as, *I hope you will find this attractive and...* rather than make a real case for their being a genuine commercial proposition. So, while the idea, the title, and the details presented are all important, come the moment when a writer types a letter to an editor, what they often seem to allow to predominate is just their "hope" that something they believe in will suit.

Given the competition to be published, anything unprofessional is likely to guarantee rejection. A powerful case must be made. What counts is good work, well presented. And "well presented" always means accurately presented. It may need to be unusual too and it certainly needs to do more than hope.

Again and again

Repetition is a classic enhancer of memory. Repetition is a classic... enough, point made. For confirmation, just look at the number of times you see the same advertisements on the television. So, the more times you can mention a book or your work the more likely it is to assist your promotion and sale of it; frankly, opportunities are likely to give out before repetition becomes annoying.

One way to increase the number of mentions of your book is to start mentioning it before it is published and available. By all means, wait until your publisher is absolutely sure when copies will be available (in one year I had one book postponed, in three or four delays, by some ten months!). But, once you are sure, start telling people about it, by mailings, by email and more. You can use some impressive material to augment the bald statement: publishers usually have a fact sheet about a title available several months before publication, and often the cover is available too. This latter is so useful it is worth suggesting, chasing and requesting copies, which can then either be physically sent to you or sent as an email attachment allowing you to print out as many copies as you wish (and perhaps add your own sales pitch to the reverse side).

Forbidden Planet is one (science fiction) bookshop that displays future covers on a regular basis in London's Shaftsbury Avenue. Others may do this too, and certainly when I look at the display of covers in this one, there are many other people doing the same thing. So, why not suggest to your local shops that they do the same, making space at least for yours? It is a proven technique that increases exposure.

"No worries"

Writing collaboratively is an option that can extend market opportunities. We all have a certain range in our writing, but working with someone else—co-authoring—can mean that we can do more than we might do solo. Various arrangements are possible. Things can be done on a 50/50 basis, or with each person doing different things and one being the major player. For example, I have written books where chapters were shared between two writers and others where one did the lion's share, but the second contribution was vital. Sometimes it is possible to do this in a way that presents little problem: we know the other person, they live or work down the road and organising the necessary liaison is entirely straightforward. On other occasions, we may reject the possibility of a potential collaboration because circumstances seem to make for difficulties. Certainly I have not pursued some such opportunities because of apparent complications.

However, I have changed my mind. Following a chance meeting with someone who lives and works in Australia, we evolved a project on which we could work jointly. I arranged publication of a book with a U.K. publisher and we have worked on the manuscript together. Messages, thoughts and ideas, then whisked their way across the globe to and from our respective computers. So too, in due course, did chunks of draft text. A clear—and agreed—brief meant that, with little or no hassle, a final manuscript was sent to the publisher. The only distraction was the visions of beautiful beaches and wonderful weather that came into my mind every time I pressed "Send" to email my colleague on the other side of the world. I just wish the finances of the project had allowed a visit! It was a profitable collaboration; and was one that will make me think differently about such things in future. Is anyone out there looking for a collaborator?

If you want to know the result, it is titled, *Why Entrepreneurs should eat Bananas* and is published by Cyan Books (Marshall Cavendish).

Two headed creativity

Much of the advice in these pages urges caution in dealing with editors. They know what they want, are fickle and, above all, they are busy. Writers are cautioned to keep their distance, not demand reasons for rejection, and certainly not poke them with the proverbial stick with the horse's head handle; it will only annoy them. It's fair comment too and, assuredly, care is necessary. But, there may be exceptions.

All my experience in the business world indicates that the old maxim "two heads are better than one" is very often true. Ideas may come from people who put an ice pack on their heads and sit quietly waiting for inspiration to strike, but more often they come from discussion, debate and interaction between people. This is as true in the world of writing as it is anywhere else. Of necessity, writing can be a solitary occupation and I have mentioned here before the advantages of networking with others to assist what you both do. But editors are human too: yes, really! And the same techniques can work for them. I have written many (non-fiction) books and about a third of them have followed meetings with editors at which no specific topic was on the table. Both parties wanted new books: me to write, them to publish and sell. Ideas were bounced around, digressions were allowed, one thing led to another until an idea appeared that seemed good for both of us. Sometimes an idea was then good enough for the next stage to be writing a synopsis that led straight to approval. Or a synopsis might need some degree of modification first.

In either case, perhaps approval came more readily because the editor was involved. It was "our idea", rather than mine. So, be careful, yes—but sometimes agreement can come this way.

Hiding your light

I attended a book launch. Not a grand do, 30-40 people, wine and nibbles in one of London's largest independent bookshops; but certainly useful. There was a good display of the new book and a fair number of copies signed and sold. The event had taken some organising: an approach to the shop by another author (living nearby), a meeting to settle details, a trip to the supermarket for food and drink and liaison with the publisher and their local representative to ensure the stock was there on time. The author had taken a useful initiative and, on the day, people arrived and enjoyed themselves; the shop manager, too, was well pleased.

But when, half an hour in and things were nicely under way, I said to the book's author, "Are you going to say a few words?" They muttered that they had not planned to do so and that the event "was better kept low key". I suspect this was not because an objective assessment of the usefulness of so doing showed it to be unnecessary, but rather because they just did not see themselves as a public speaker, despite missing an opportunity. Yet you never know who will be at such an event. To prepare a few words does not take long, and maybe it would have made a useful event more useful still. If lack of confidence or skill in such a thing prevents it happening, it diminishes a writer's armoury of ways of making themselves successful in the market. No such initiative should be allowed to be stillborn or diluted because an element of it goes by default due to lack of skill or thought. In the same way that you cannot be "a bit pregnant", any promotion must be truly effective or all the time and effort of doing it is wasted. Even if it means acquiring new skills, the effect should surely be maximised.

Productivity rules O.K.

When writing for money, effectively everything you write is paid for at so much per word. Your editor may not say this literally, but being paid say £100 for a 1000 word article, means 10p a word. And if you did that in just an hour then, head down, you could earn £700 in a day doing seven such articles—and still break for lunch and the odd cup of tea. Sadly, of course, it does not work like that.

Alternatively, imagine that you take a full day to complete such an article. Say seven hours (let's ignore the cups of tea). Then you earn less than £15 per hour. So productivity matters. For example, when I first began to write my column, I found it somewhat difficult to hit the exact word count. Adding to, subtracting from or altering what I had written extended the writing time. But practice led to a situation where I could normally get within ten words either way on my first try. So writing time is effectively reduced. What actually happens, of course, is not automatic; rather improvement occurs through conscious striving. Practice needs working at, if it is to be useful.

What is true for a small batch of words is true for the whole writing process. Many a writer wanting to earn significant money from their craft can benefit from attention to their productivity. The more your approach to writing helps you complete tasks without undue delay or digression (though, of course, you do need to think carefully about what you deliver), the better your hourly rate will be and the more time you have to write other things—and boost your earnings further.

Brass neck

A magazine editor once told me about a really unusual experience. His telephone rang and he was told that there was someone in Reception waiting to see him. He was not expecting anyone and, having asked the name, was none the wiser—it meant nothing to him. He asked what they wanted. "He won't say, but promises that he won't keep you more than 60 seconds," the Receptionist told him. This was unusual: people did not usually turn up without any arrangement and this oddity was compounded by the refusal to explain.

Intrigued, he arranged for the man to come to his office. Asking what he could do for him, prompted his visitor to produce a book and explain that his first book was to be published in three weeks' time—he wanted the editor to feature a review of it. He also apologised for his tactics, touched on his promise to be no more than 60 seconds and handed over a fact sheet about the book along with a disc on which were a photograph of the author and the book's cover.

At this point, still intrigued, the editor did spend a few minutes with him and later got a review written, which was duly published in the magazine. He mentioned the story to me, simply because it was so unusual; "No one has ever approached me like that before," he said. The sheer effrontery was sufficient for the author to get what he wanted (and, yes, if you are wondering, the review was good).

Now I do *not* recommend this wholesale; but I do recommend the principle. Even today, with most authors able to study the essentials of what makes for successful promotion, there is room for something bold and unusual—and it can work. Now you could...

Time spent in reconnaissance

Know your market. This good advice appears frequently in these pages, but ultimately markets mean people: individuals like the busy editor that your proposal will be sent to or whose desk it will find its way onto. You need to know them too. Certainly it is better to find out who it is most appropriate to communicate with in a particular company and a simple telephone call, perhaps going no further than the switchboard, may suffice to obtain that information. But what else can you do?

The answer can be expressed in one word: research. A prime source of current information about the publishing field is the trade press; for those interested in publishing books this is *The Bookseller* and *Publishing News*. Here you will get a glimpse into the future. Information about what new books are due to be published is a major part of their content. This alone may help as your idea for a book may be best directed as a logical match for an earlier book, for example as an addition to a series or something designed to build on recent success.

In addition there is news about people. Who is joining what company? Who is being promoted or taking on new responsibility? What new imprints are being started? What are people saying about prospects? More personal news has a place here too. It may help couch a proposal in the right terms to know how old someone is or that they handle another specific author.

Time spent in reconnaissance is seldom wasted, as they say in the military. Getting into print and making money from it needs a systematic approach. Proceeding on the basis of up to date, pertinent information (and perhaps information that other, less conscientious, authors do not have) can only help. Maybe one additional fact can make the difference between receiving another rejection slip and success.

Something to aim for

The deadline for my column ("Going to market", from which this is adapted) is imposed on me (and very welcome it is too, Mr Editor). As such it becomes a target, and I must respect it if I want to continue writing my pieces. It is also possible to set personal targets for yourself. Given the nature of the job of getting published, this is perhaps very sensible.

Getting published is a numbers game. You have to put enough bread on the waters, you have to speculate to accumulate, you have to... enough. Suffice to say, there is a direct relationship between the volume of things you do (yes, provided they are well chosen and executed) and the likelihood of success. You do not have to read any magazine for writers for long to appreciate that the statistics involved are less than favourable. Sending one letter is thus somewhat unlikely to get you a contract, much less instant fame and fortune. So how can you motivate yourself to do more?

Set some targets. All sorts of things will help. Resolve to send one enquiry letter every week—or better still every day. Resolve to contact a potential agent every month or every week. Keep records. When you do what you planned, tick a box, award yourself a gold star or a large gin and tonic. But regard your activity plan as mandatory, and when the commitment is achieved think about what you can do next. Always look ahead, set more targets and stick to those too. Tell yourself that every single extra prospecting action you take increases your chances of generating interest, and of getting agreement—because it does.

To tinker with an old Arabic proverb: *If you want to do something (i.e., get published) you find a way. If you don't want to do anything, you find an excuse.*

There are more, different, thought-provokers in the next chapter.

9 An on-going process—keep thinking

> *Ideas are like rabbits. You get a couple and learn how to handle them, and pretty soon you have dozens.*
>
> John Steinbeck

No preambles: this chapter continues with more of the short, catalyst-type thoughts of the last chapter, further demonstrating that success is in the detail, in both attitude and action. I would just mention, though, that splitting this list into two chapters gives the book ten chapters, and there are those that feel such a number affects the likelihood of turning browsing into actual purchase. And that's fine with me; I want to leave no stone unturned in maximizing sales. Back to the list…

Being useful

An email flags a message from a publisher: asking if I can take over and write a planned book, substituting for an author who, through illness, cannot complete a commission? It is an attractive offer, unexpected, and at first I am tempted. But the book is quite long, the deadline rather short and my immediate future workload is somewhat hectic, so I regretfully decline (and contrive to be helpful by suggesting a colleague).

This opportunity came to nothing, but was still pleasing. Why? Not just because it was flattering to be considered, though to be honest it was, but also because it demonstrated that the publisher saw me in the right light. First, they had a clear note of the kind of writing I do, one that seemed to be broader than the topics I have actually written about for them (and others) and included the fact that I have ghost written books before. It is very easy to get typecast, known only for a narrow range of things that a particular publisher sees directly. Opportunities, however, may arise in other areas and, only if you have made a point of informing contacts more broadly, are they able to think of you when they have a project in search of a writer. Furthermore, such information must be kept up to date, and contacts reminded and re-reminded of your existence and of your competencies. Systematic networking activity can pay dividends.

Even when, as here, an enquiry is not suitable (and thus actually not useful to you) it is still best to be helpful—suggesting another name as I did in this case, or whatever. Now two contacts are reminded to think of me as helpful, and next time when they say, *Who might write this or knows someone who could?* they may well say, *Patrick?* And next time it may suit.

Don't delay

Following a palpable success with her first book, Donna Tart waited ten years before publishing her next. For many writers, such a gap would not just be an indulgence, it could spell financial catastrophe. For those who make their living by writing, either in whole or part, work done and money paid for it must be regular events. Where writing is a business, productivity and cash flow can be constant worries.

It is a well established principle in the business world that it is easier to sell something to a past customer, at least to a satisfied one, than to find a new prospect. So too, surely, with writing: yet many writers seem curiously reticent about what, elsewhere, would be basic follow-up contact. If, say, an article is accepted, if the editor likes it, schedules it for publication and will pay for it, then surely the likelihood of their taking more from the same author increases. Editors take a risk whenever they commission something. Will it arrive on spec and on time? Will it be of similar quality to any specimen or past piece they saw? With a tried and tested writer, someone they have had contact with and experience of, the risk lessens.

They may not instantly commission more, but they may be more open to further ideas—right now, with a recent and satisfactory experience in mind and not lost in the hotchpotch of events that doubtless makes up their busy life. So the time to float new ideas is sooner rather than later; and that means having ideas ready to float and thinking of the longer term as soon as a contact or commission occurs. It is easy to hesitate—*let's give them a moment*—then finding the moment has passed, just when what's needed is confident, purposeful action.

Fresh opportunities

After the thrill of first publication, your book's sales will likely slow down, so too realistically will the likelihood of your seeing it prominently displayed. So you all too quickly reach the point where you may want to produce a promotional shot in the arm. One route is to obtain press mentions. Not reviews, the time for that will pass and it is difficult to get anything other than a new book reviewed.

So you need stories, and you need to tell the press about them in the right way. Check out exactly how a Press Release should be written, because the form is as important as the content. (I explained this briefly in Chapter 6). Compile a list of suitable publications; here you can aim nationwide or more locally. Think what you might say and write about it clearly, attractively and persuasively. Stories might be about you—*Author moves to Anytown*—*Author available to talk about their writing*—*Author visits local library*. Or there may be things to say about the book—*Now to appear in Hungarian*—*Author creates Asian edition of their book*—*Dog eats book*; whatever.

Success can lead to publicity and such mentions give you something else to use for further publicity; for example, maybe your local library or bookshop will post a cutting on their noticeboard.

Finally, consider giving your story a postscript (in italics/brackets perhaps) suggesting that people buy the book—signed?—direct from the author. Strangely, many publishing contracts seem to prohibit authors buying books for resale. But do check this, most publishers are in fact happy to see any additional sales and the discount they give you may allow a promotional gesture, for example free postage, and produce you some extra profit. And if income from one book continues to accrue, it may encourage you to write the next!

All's fair

Writing is a business. Well, certainly I assume that if you are reading this then you want to make money at it. Publishing is a business too. No one who has ever stepped into the London Book Fair could be in any doubt of that. It is a large exhibition. When I went, there were plenty of visitors, indeed it was difficult to walk down the aisles or onto some of the stands.

As I mentioned in the last chapter, an old military saying says that *time spent in reconnaissance is seldom wasted*. In my view, the need for research is strong, and there can be few ways in which research can be done more quickly than regular reading of both *Writing Magazine* and similar publications in print and on line. It can be difficult to get time with editorial staff (and difficult to make an appointment) at the exhibition, but it is a good place to see what publishers do and how they present themselves. Simple observation can show you where your book might fit, and where it definitely does not. It is also a good place to discover names—identifying the right person to send your precious manuscript to once the dust has settled. I suspect that the two-three weeks after the show, and after the Frankfurt Book Fair too, is the worst possible time to communicate with publishers as they struggle to recover after the hectic days on the stand.

Overall, the force with which a visitor to the Fair will be reminded that publishing is a business, and a competitive and a hectic one at that, is very powerful. Next time you sit down to write to a publisher do bear this in mind. Publishers are not there to help you. They operate in whatever way will create profitability in a dynamic marketplace. But they cannot do this without authors (though some might like to!). Perhaps you will do best by aiming to show them how you can help them meet their objectives, rather than expecting them to help you achieve yours.

From record to opportunity

Sometimes while searching for opportunities, one comes to you. An editor rang me. Their magazine's 100th edition was due, I had had an article in the launch issue and they wanted me to revisit the subject "ten years on". 1400 words, deadline (and fee) agreed; no problem. But it made me think. With hindsight I could easily have calculated the anniversary then, if they had not asked me, I could have made a suggestion. For article writers there is a good habit to be established here, and anything that prompts opportunities from so simple a premise is to be welcomed.

Now ten years is a long time to wait between commissions and I am not suggesting you do that (besides, I had written regularly for the magazine in the interim). But "anniversary" can have a broad definition. You might like to look at it in three specific ways that may prompt further thoughts.

Firstly, there is the publication itself. An anniversary might mean something significant—five, ten years on—or it could just mean a year later. Even this simple thought prompts numbers of potential hooks on which to hang suggestions.

Secondly, add the whole question of time, seasons and events. Can you write and aim to sell something to fit logically with Christmas, Easter, summer holidays, Lent, the first cuckoo or the start of the new tax year? The possibilities here are legion.

Thirdly, there is the link between an article's topic and timing specific to that. What makes something topical? It may be 100 years since someone was born, six months since they were released from prison or rescued from a shipwreck. It may be as simple as it being their birthday. All such situations have sales possibilities; they help make suggestions notable. Now when can I revisit this topic? Next year, or…

This length or that

Question: why is *abbreviated* such a long word? Sorry, I know it's been said before, but it does get us started. One way to maximise your writing opportunities is to write on a subject at different lengths. For example, start with an article of say 2000 words; let us assume that this is the brief for a commission from a magazine. Such a length gives plenty of scope, and may well allow for a few digressions along the way. Once you have written a text with which you feel comfortable, see what else you can do with it.

Amending and reducing such an article may give you something that is suitable to submit to another prospective publisher. You might rework it in the form of 1500 words, or 1000—or both. Maybe you can encapsulate the essence of it in 100 words; indeed the *Daily Telegraph* was recently running a competition for an "extraordinary travel tale" that was restricted to just one hundred words. This is a process that presents some difficulty for many writers. Was the 2000 word version not perfect? What can you possibly omit? Yet the exercise of recasting material in this sort of way is a skill worth developing. It makes you plan the shape and structure of material, it makes you tighten the language—turning the likes of *at this moment in time* (which should perhaps not have been there in the first place) into *now*—and it makes you work hard to get over your description or message in a precise and concise manner.

If you can learn to do this effectively, then you can regard everything you write not only as a complete work in its own right, but also as the raw material for additional pieces of work and thus additional commissions.

Bread on the waters

Pop into the local shop for bread or ask the Post Office for first class stamps and you do not expect to be told to return tomorrow as they have none in stock. So too for many of the things you buy, though if you rush straight from watching *Top Gear* to buy the latest supercar, expect to wait; they build them one at a time and charge accordingly.

How does this link to writing? Well, what sort of writer are you? Some write something, try to sell it and, having sold it, write something else and the cycle continues. Others have many things on the go at the same time. Not ideas, writers need lots of those. I mean actual pieces of writing up for sale. With books, the numbers must be kept manageable, though now I think of it I have one manuscript finished and due with the publisher, another book just finished with only a final read through to go, and another on page two—some way to go with that last one. With articles the numbers may be greater.

There is no reason why you cannot have 10, 20, 100 articles out with prospective editorial buyers. Sometimes the first person you send something to buys it promptly. On other occasions you need to be patient, allow time for consideration, and approach other potential buyers if necessary. The more bread you put on the waters, as it were, the greater the chances of making sales. Certainly the one thing you can be sure of is that if you send out nothing, you will sell nothing. Work sent out and "under consideration" is the writer's equivalent of stock; and what's in stock can be sold.

Get to the marmalade

You have a great idea. It is well formed and you can see the structure of it in detail. You like it. You know it will sell. An editor may or may not share your opinion. They may buy… or not. But there is a third possibility, they seek to change it.

This can be hard. You like what you have thought through and think it right (dare one say: perfect). So your first thought is often defensive: you seek to convince them to approve the original idea. This can be fatal. Some writers are lucky enough to write and sell exactly what they like. More often, especially with non-fiction, the job is to match something with a stated brief. This includes a simple level such as hitting the required word count for instance. But it may also involve more. I have just completed a book that, to fit the style of a series, had to be in ten chapters with each chapter having six standard features, such as a particular kind of introductory paragraph. There is nothing wrong with this, indeed its role in defining the series is important, but it is not what I would have chosen. Indeed it probably took a little longer to write than something on the same subject in a different style.

So be it; as my mother used to say: given oranges, the job is to make marmalade. You must deliver what is required. So, whenever discussions lead away from your original idea, see that as a positive step towards agreement—coming to a consensus can give you a job. And it is just possible that the editor knows what will sell better than you do!

Cards on the table

If you write and aim to sell your writing do you have a business card? If not, you are not alone. Yet you will know (I claim no originality here) the saying about success coming not from what you know, but rather from who you know. Contacts are potentially invaluable, and business cards are a core tool of networking, the modern term for making contact and keeping in touch.

Even in other spheres of business, people are often remiss here. I spoke to a number of people at a business event recently and when I asked for a card was told by several that they either did not have one or did not have one with them. Surely this is easy enough to organise and, remember, various internet sites offer such cheaply or even for free.

Over the years I have fortuitously met people such as publishers, writers, magazine editors and others who have proved valuable ongoing contacts or who, in turn, have introduced me to further useful people. I have co-written with some, ghost written for others and collaborated with still more in a variety of ways. I spoke to a writing group and a local Rotary Club, both organised following chance meetings. Unless I had given them a card it might have been much easier for them to forget their intention.

So, if you do not have a business card, get one. Get one soon. Then keep them by you and dish them out with abandon, following-up if necessary to maintain contact. You never know which new contacts may prove useful or profitable, but you can be sure that some will be.

Never standard

If you write part-time and work at other things, then you may have a curriculum vitae (CV)—a career resume. Such need a degree of individuality, yet to be effective should also fit a form; giving recipients what they expect. But there is one key piece of advice about them: a CV is *not* a standard document. It must be tailored to its use; send it to a particular prospective employer and you may sensibly need to emphasise some aspects and play down or omit others. It takes a moment, but changes it from trying to be all things to all people to being right for one particular job.

So too with what you say about yourself as a writer: firstly, you may need different versions just to produce different lengths of text—not everyone wants your life history. Secondly, you need to vary the way you describe different aspects of your experience and achievements. For example, I write books, articles and other things such as text for websites and corporate publications. I write on a mixture of topics, from business to travel, and have ghost written books, co-written books, edited books and... enough about me. The point is that what I say about these different things needs to be varied, depending on how relevant each may be for an individual approach. Sometimes an item warrants detailed description. Sometimes it only warrants a brief word or should be omitted altogether, though I always put that "I write a regular column for *Writing Magazine*!" You can work from one version to the next, keeping copies of several to save time. If a tailored version impresses, then the necessary editing and rewriting is time well spent.

New forever?

Most authors want to maximise sales, and most too would accept that, in part, sales are down to what they do and cannot be left entirely to publishers or good fortune. The moment of having a book published is clearly a unique opportunity to seek and gain some publicity. There are all sorts of things you can do to support whatever a publisher does on launch, but it is all contained within a brief period. Nothing is new forever. Or is it?

Sticking with books (articles have similar possibilities), there are in fact potentially many "new" moments to which you can link publicity. The publication of a hardback book is the beginning. Then there is the large format paperback, the mass market-sized paperback, new editions (I have one book in its fifth incarnation), new covers, and translations into foreign languages. The latter potentially has two dimensions: even if the opportunities of assisting publicity for, say, a Spanish edition, are minimal, maybe it warrants a press release at home that will draw attention to the original English edition. Having said that, with non-fiction books, I have had foreign editions prompt an opportunity to visit the country concerned, for instance to attend and speak at a conference. Long-term, a further opportunity may occur when a book goes out of print and is published again by a different publisher. Similarly, if self-publication makes it possible to interest a publisher, then there will be another launch.

Sometimes what occurs just happens; though it is up to the author to take advantage of it. On other occasions, opportunities occur because the author has actively and successfully persuaded a publisher to take a certain course of action.

Seasonal sense

The concept of supporting your writing promotionally is well established in these pages. But what do you do? What's worthwhile? Some opportunities present themselves and decisions about them can be difficult.

Let me look back to Christmas for an example. A nearby branch of a major chain of bookshops held a "local authors evening" in the approach to Christmas; would I participate? Yes, I said, I would. On the due date, seven or eight people assembled at the shop, which closed as usual then reopened at 7pm with a bevy of tables set around the ground floor with an eager author sitting at each behind a pile of books. During the ensuing hour, only a dozen people entered the shop and only one local author sold a book: a single copy to another author!

The reasons perhaps include inadequate publicity, timing and customers being unaware of the late night opening in the town; this started in the evening, but few people were about. No matter. Was it a waste of time? I think not. Firstly, some things did come of it: conversations with staff led to a commitment to hold a different event that I think will work much better and I met another author with whom collaboration may be possible at another event. Secondly, there is no way of knowing, in advance, whether such an event will be useful or not. And some work very well. Coincidentally, I gave a talk at a golf club on the previous evening that was well worthwhile.

Invitations are not so many (for most writers) that you should not take a chance. What matters is the rate of strike and influencing matters as much as possible along the way.

What's in a title?

I am commissioned to write a book about managing your career (in an organisation). I thought I had the perfect title for this, but when the editor phoned to confirm the project she said that they were unsure about the title, "We'll do some checking", she said. They did too. The sales director was canvassed, so was the managing director, the publicity person, the publishing director and, for all I know, the receptionist and the guy who delivers sandwiches at lunchtime. An email went to their distributor in America and the export manager was doubtless consulted. At least three completely different titles were considered, plus various subtitles, and how they would link to cover design was also reviewed.

Make no mistake, I have no objection to this; titles are important and when a book is published it may make a difference to how it sells, both to the trade and off the shelves once it is in the shops. Similarly, magazine articles often have serious consideration given to titles and it can well be the editor's version that appears rather than the author's choice. What does all this mean for the author? Well, I for one always head a synopsis or suggestion with the words "Working title" to make it clear that I expect—welcome—discussion and perhaps change. If I can think of good alternatives I put in two or three. I believe this helps show a flexible and professional approach and assists my relationship with editors.

That said, some titles sound odd initially, for example there is a book called *Bombproof your horse* (which no longer sounds odd when you find it is about training horses to keep calm in noisy and difficult situations). But what about my careers book? They settled on *Disaster-proof your career*, which I hope will do the job.

Frequency

I have a new client: a magazine. My first article appears in their current issue and they have taken more. Given the frequency of the magazine, the editor will not want something from me every five minutes, nor to hear from me too often either. They have demonstrated, however, that they work well in advance, indeed that they are prepared to commission a piece far ahead of publication date. So, if I am to make them someone who takes my writing regularly, I must consider the flow of communications between us.

Whatever the circumstances, this is always important. Put something aside and it can be forgotten. Leave too long a gap and the moment passes and, when you do re-contact people, you generate only silence or a "no". But you do need a plan: if you keep a record (or file) about such a contact—and you should—then the last entry should not be a record, it should be a commitment. As I said in Chapter 2, it should say when you plan to re-contact them and how. Such a date will sometimes be a week ahead; or a month, or two. But you need the certainty of having made a considered decision about what you will do next in writing; preferably linked to your diary too (if you are not a dinosaur like me, then this might well be on your computer).

Ring the changes too. My last contact with the editor above was a meeting. I made suggestions by email and submitted my copy that way too. What next? Do I write, email, telephone or try to organise another meeting? Whatever I do, it should be planned and executed to maximise the chances of maintaining and developing the business.

An endangered species

Sometimes writers get letters from readers. It is good to feel someone—anyone—has read your deathless prose, especially if their feedback is positive, but one thing always upsets me. That is when people say, "I got your book from the library"… when I want people to buy them!

That said, libraries are often great assets for authors: they may have display areas where local authors can post details of their books, indeed they may even have a system for stocking and selling them (mine takes 30% commission). And, even more useful, they may run various events. In my local library, these range from readings by authors of children's books to talks about writing, getting published or the topic of particular books. These are run both independently and also linked in to such events as local literary festivals.

Setting up something like this may only need a suggestion based on something you observe ("…perhaps I might do something like your event on 18 August?"), or it may need a number of contacts making suggestions and following them up over some months. So be it, the end result can be worthwhile: both "on the day" and with things like an announcement or a report in the press. Always, too, one thing can lead to another; someone sees what you are doing and contacts you about other possibilities. I did a talk at my local library this morning. I sold some books, the Librarian promised to remember me for other things, I met three other interesting authors, was photographed for the local paper and got my book cover in the library display case. It was certainly worthwhile—the tea and biscuits were good too.

Changing habits

Recently, I wrote something for a publisher with guidelines forbidding the use of the word "key". Given that what I was writing was aimed at readers in the business world, this is a word that tends to crop up regularly: key issues, key objectives and more.

The instruction made me think. I checked another recent manuscript, clicking on "Find" and listing the key (sic) word. I was amazed how many times it appeared in a manuscript of, I think, 40,000 words. Alongside this, I began to think of alternatives. I looked up "crucial" in my thesaurus (something every writer should have and use regularly) and went on from there. Soon I had listed many alternatives—pivotal, critical, central, significant and more—many of which, with precise and slightly different meanings, substituted for "key" in a way that was more appropriate, and made the writing stronger and better. I duly avoided the word "key" in the piece of writing in question and resolved to double-check its appropriateness every time I was tempted to use it elsewhere in future.

Writers easily get set in their ways. What we deliver matters and this mattering may include just a single word. But making what we write suit each commissioner is what gets work accepted and what gets us sufficiently well thought of to get agreement to write more. I have written here previously about productivity, but precision matters too. It took me longer to write at length avoiding the word "key", but that was what was needed. Even when such is not prescribed, we must get every detail right if someone is going to say not just that they like it, but also that they will pay for it.

Buddying up

The idea of writing buddies is a good one. Certainly, discussions and debate with others can positively affect your quality of writing; it is a useful activity best done regularly. But collaboration possibilities do not stop there. Some things can be co-authored too, and there is another whole area of possible collaboration.

If you can benefit from writing in a way that compares notes with others, then the same can be done with the marketing of work. Sometimes this can be on what is essentially a one-off basis; for instance, I have more than once worked with people to find a publisher, earning myself a small percentage of their advance when a successful arrangement was made. But more useful, and perhaps more pleasant too given the solitary nature of writing, is a regular liaison, one that maybe combines conferring about writing as well as discussing sales possibilities.

In such relationships, you may be able to swap contacts (or make specific introductions), exchange notes about how editors have reacted to something, or from observation suggest good moments to make contact with someone (maybe suggesting adding a book to a series or writing an article for a forthcoming special edition of a magazine). Any combination of people, in terms of writing experience and success, can work together, but maybe it works best when one at least has some record of publication success. Broader networks are possible too as a third or fourth person joins in. If you are the one without experience, don't worry it may still work well: your more experienced partner may still be pleased to have a collaborator and besides your experience may soon start to catch up!

How much?

Much of what I write here might be said to involve the word "struggle". The struggle to get published, please editors, get paid—all are uncertain and time-consuming and sometimes the return, a small payment for a short article, seems meagre.

But sometimes things go well. This may be a one-off; I once won a place on a writing course worth the best part of £500 for a 50 word short story. Or it may be really worthwhile, though nothing is forever, and one of the best deals in terms of word count and money that I have had was with a magazine that closed down.

Sometimes too, success may be a real surprise and, surprisingly, that can pose problems too. Again an example from my experience illustrates. I was sitting in an editor's office. He had agreed I should write a book for them and when I asked if there would be an advance he named a figure three times my best hope. I was amazed—delighted. But, at the same time, I was immediately determined not to show it. Surely a professional writer should be used to such sums I thought. My reaction had to be impassive. I wanted to jump up and shout, but I quelled all visible signs of delight and said, in what I hoped was a matter of fact tone, "Right, that seems fine".

Mostly, when writing something for someone for the first time, you will want to do more writing in the future. And, in this case, I did not want my reaction to mean I got offered half as much on any repeat assignment. So don't overdo the gratitude on acceptance. Think ahead, think quickly and save the ecstasy for later.

The right moment

It is often said in these pages that a rejection is not necessarily a sign of poor writing, only that something is not right for whoever it has been sent to. Or that whatever was sent arrived at the wrong moment. Conversely, if you can pick the right moment, exactly the right moment, then the reaction may be favourable.

Now you cannot know what is going on at the other end or whether an editor is having a bad day, but there is another factor—you can pick a moment when something is topical. If the topicality also injects an element of urgency into the equation, then that is so much the better. For example, in one particular July, I submitted an idea for a (non-fiction) book on a topic that had suddenly become topical—the details don't matter—to two publishers. One said, "interesting", then, "no". The second said, "good idea" and then, "yes". What is significant is that the approach, sent by email, consisted of a line and half; not much more than twenty words. No full proposal, no synopsis—but the appeal of the topical nature was such that, with only a paragraph or two more added to describe the book, we moved straight to a contract. The contract demanded delivery by the end of August (only five weeks ahead); I rapidly arranged to co-write the book, to share the load, and the manuscript was delivered on time.

I describe all this because I think it illustrates something interesting about the way publishers work. Find the right thing at the right moment and the chances of getting agreement are heightened and apparently heightened to a considerable extent. Now what else is going to hit a high of topicality?

The power of the blurb

I have just delivered a book manuscript (on time) and, as is my habit, the second page after the title page was the blurb—suggested copy for the back cover. It was headed "Draft blurb", and may well be subject to discussion or change (I would not want the publisher to think I was arrogantly expecting it to be automatically accepted). But I do feel that the best person to write such a draft is a book's author. After all, who knows it better?

That said, let me make two points about this. Firstly, perhaps especially for a non-fiction book, writing the blurb and writing it up front, ahead of, or early on in the writing of a book, concentrates the mind. You want the book to sell, so you must surely be able to describe it to someone in a way that makes it sound attractive. Doing so can direct the content and affect the way you write. For example, my manuscript mentioned above is a book aimed at students. In the blurb, it states that the book presents useful information in "a highly accessible" way. Bearing this in mind, there were occasions during the writing when I checked descriptions with other people, made amendments and the final text was, I believe, better—and more saleable—for that.

Secondly, I will want to do what I can to assist the publisher prompt sales and the first step is surely to think through the book, its potential market and what should make it appeal to readers. Writing the blurb prompts you to do just that. It's an important early step to linking what you have published with the market—and seeing it sell well.

Thankfully memorable

It is always nice when someone says, "Thank you". The modern world seems less concerned about this and many things, including birthday presents, dinner invitations and more, go unacknowledged, or only prompt a quick telephone call or text. The written thank you, whether letter or card, seems largely consigned to history.

Such is life, but there are two good reasons for writers to buck this trend. Firstly, there is the simple satisfaction of saying thank you and the impact that doing so has on others and the relationships between you. Secondly, there is the opportunity to do this and make it a constructive communication, one that moves a situation forward. There are plenty of opportunities: when your article is published, when your new book drops on the doormat, when you are paid—all deserve a thank you. What better moment to pursue other ideas and to make suggestions—a new book, a new topic for an article, a new edition or a request to meet. Maybe such deserves a letter, yes an old-fashioned letter; bear in mind that an email can be deleted in a split second (though some writers define a split second as the time between their suggestion landing on someone's desk and their deciding to reject it!).

Making such communications constructive is a useful opportunity. There is an awful American expression to the effect that if you can fake the sincerity, everything else is easy. I am certainly not advocating this level of cynicism. It is obviously best to offer genuine and pleasantly delivered thanks, but there is surely no harm in then incorporating this into the chain of communications with a publisher and making it a part of your sales strategy.

Dear Author

Whatever you write, books or articles, you may occasionally get letters from readers; perhaps more than occasionally. Ignoring the ones in green ink that suggest you do something distasteful or physically impossible, and possibly those— which I hate—that start by saying that they borrowed your book from the library, making me want to reply with no more than "Buy a copy!", what are you to do with them?

Mostly you should reply. If you have something to sell, then an "If you've read that, why not buy this?" response regards them as customers; though, however flattering their letter and however nice they sound, get a cheque first. Remember the old saying—it's not an order until the money's in the bank! You may be able to reply by email (postage costs enough to be a worry these days), and however you reply, to save time, you can probably start with some standard text electronically stored. Be polite, sound pleased to hear from them and remember that if they like your reply they may tell others about it and this can prompt more sales. With articles, it may be worth telling an editor if people communicate with you direct; signs of your material being appreciated may help prompt other commissions. These days it is pretty easy to have some material to send, especially by email. For example, adding an attachment showing the cover of a (nother) book may well act to prompt orders.

Occasionally a reader will write more than once. One lady has now contacted me five times about the same book, each time buying several copies, which she apparently likes to give as gifts—now *that* I'm certainly at pains to encourage.

You know it's coming

A theme that consistently sells is topicality. Some of this is hung round things like an anniversary. You can write an article linked to the 100th anniversary of a famous person's birth, or of a building or whatever and it can be planned well in advance. You know the due date and can send something to a magazine in good time for the issue concurrent with the event; either a query letter or a suggested article. Providing nothing is already commissioned, an editor can schedule it in and know that a little space is appropriately filled.

But not everything can be planned ahead. Yet newspapers and magazines often follow a seemingly sudden event with a related feature very promptly.

It was the physicist, Niels Bohr who said that, "prediction is always difficult, especially of the future". Maybe: but actually some things really *are* predictable and, as such, represent opportunities for you to place this kind of feature. What prompted me to think about this was a parliamentary row, an MP was sanctioned for being rude and, the day after, an article appeared in the *Daily Telegraph* about the art of insults. Now this almost comes into the category I mean: certainly you can be pretty sure that there will be more such rudeness and probably before too long. So many things *can be* anticipated: without any doubt there will be a new version of the iPad launched, a period of exceptional weather (flooding say), an earthquake, a train crash, an incident of perfect customer service or a... but you get the idea.

The trick is to have something ready for when it does happen, add in a link—and act fast.

Instant sale

Marketers talk about "impulse buys", products that sell because something—that is something they plan—triggers the customer to say, "Oh let's get that!" even though it was an unplanned purchase. It works; which of us has never picked up some chocolate at the cash point on a whim?

It works with books too. Books displayed face out in a bookshop are more likely to sell than those showing only their spine, and those in piles face up on table displays do even better. So most authors seeing their book in a shop will surreptitiously alter the display to this effect; certainly I do this unashamedly. A different prompt to impulse buying is the author's talk. Again, I certainly plug my book, judiciously of course, when I give talks.

The opportunities for this sort of prompt are legion. Another one—linked to new technology—starts with the humble newsletter. I recently experienced an example: I received a new newsletter emailed from American novelist, Timothy Hallinan (excellent thrillers set in Thailand!). In it he explained that he had returned to an early work, a private detective novel long out of print, reworked it and was offering it for sale as an e-book. Well, loving his books, my £2.16 was winging its way to Amazon in a moment and with one click. Amazon's commission in such circumstances is pretty modest so, even at low, purchase-prompting prices, this is an excellent way to increase earnings. For a writer, any prompting of impulse buys can be well worthwhile. Furthermore my £2.16 was well spent. Regarding *The man with no time*, I was hooked from page one!

Formal member

How did your last writing assignment originate? Approaches you make may come from many sources: observation (noticing a new magazine), from a meeting (an event like the London Book Fair or a Literary Festival) or from formal indications about publishers' activities and requirements in such as the *Writers' News* supplement, now promoted into the main magazine; something I find useful and which has regularly led to assignments. Naturally, not every approach or query bears fruit—some fall on stony ground or take a long time to germinate. But what matters is the success rate. Something confirmed today is good and then it matters little how long ago the initiative started. All this might be called research—identifying possibilities—and, in sales jargon, prospecting—that is taking a variety of initiatives. And all, or much of it, is a solitary task.

I have commended collaboration in various ways before, and remain in favour of writing groups, co-writing, writing "buddies" and more; all can accelerate experience and success. But, let's be hard-nosed about this, sometimes such things can be social and time-consuming; they are fun but may not help the prospecting. Success is not guaranteed of course, but nothing beats liaison with fellow published writers and that may need a specific tactic. After speaking at a conference of the Society of Women Writers & Journalists, I was prevailed upon to become a member (and, yes, as I said before, there are a minority of men who are members!).

I attended their AGM. It was interesting, fun and, because the meeting was set for tea time, the scones were great. But everyone had a business hat on too and I am now pursuing some leads. Perhaps I will see you at a future meeting.

Not your bag?

From what you have read so far here, I hope I come over as a reasonably competent writer. I hope it's clear that I have some experience of the publishing world, of getting and being published and, not unimportant, getting paid for it. But there are areas where I have little expertise and one of those is cooking. I can make bacon and eggs and do toast simultaneously. I have a small repertoire of things I make perfectly, if you like porridge and custard made so that the spoon stands upright. But that's it.

So I did not immediately leap with joy when one publisher, having turned down my every suggestion, ended by saying that the area of their list they really wanted to expand was… cook books. Nothing for me there then; or was there? I thought for a moment. I have worked regularly around South East Asia over the years and have friends there. One friend used to manage a hotel and is a professional cook. She has always wanted to write a cookbook but her English is rather like Winnie-the-Pooh's spelling—wobbly. She is expressive enough, but could not deliver sufficiently good written English.

I put it to her; 100 or more recipes? No problem. I suggested to the publisher that I would act as an editor-cum-translator and we did a deal. I have ghost written books in the past and this is simpler, just de-wobbling her turn of phrase.

The project might never have happened; now it will be the only book of its sort published in the U.K. actually written by a Thai national (the book is *Everyday Thai Cookery*).

It just goes to show that we writers can turn our hands to many things that have a cheque attached. It pays to think laterally.

Careful of mismatched opinions

They say that you know you are getting older when the policemen look younger, but there are other signs too and I came across one recently as I delivered a manuscript and received a (small!) number of queries from the editor.

My contact is recent. My regular contact at the publisher concerned is on maternity leave. Every time such a change occurs, the new incumbent seems younger; as much a sign of my advancing age as anything, I'm sure. But why I mention it is because she queried the quotations I had carefully chosen and placed at the head of chapters in a book aimed at university students. One was from Vidal Sassoon, *The only place success comes before work is in the dictionary*, and another, if I remember right, was said by Oscar Wilde. Now I love quotations: a clever, succinct point, sometimes with a humorous edge, is a proven way to extend learning and get readers to remember something (and the book was a how-to text). But my editor was adamant and insisted that "students will not know these people" and felt that readers might thus be alienated by their inclusion.

I disagree. I thought, and still do, that such a device at the start of a chapter can work well regardless of whether readers know the quoted author or not. But wait a minute: both the editor and the readers aimed at are a good bit younger than me and I have to bear this in mind. Ultimately, I am paid to deliver what the editor wants. I might argue such a point, but the final decision is with the publisher (at least if I want to go on working for them).

It always pays to know your customer, and maybe such an age gap is just one more thing for a writer to think about if they want work published.

As I said early on, the last two chapters have not aimed at comprehensiveness, nor would that be possible in terms of all the ideas that might be useful. The principle here is important however—thinking about what you do and how you do it should be a constant preoccupation of the writer-for-hire. So, before I end, let me add just a few more thoughts in a last, short chapter.

Into the future: sex, writing and financial success

> *Someday I hope to write a book where the royalties will pay for the copies I give away.*
>
> Clarence Darrow

When Stephen Hawking's book *A Brief History of Time* was being published, he was told that every mathematical equation it contained risked halving its sales. He risked including only one and the book became a considerable bestseller. Similarly I have always been told that books sell more if they have the word sex on the contents page. Hence the heading above, which allows me to meet that criteria and gives me another small way to reinforce my message that success is in the details, though, sorry, that's the only relevance of the word here.

This short concluding chapter might better be called an afterword. It adds no new ideas; rather it commends a particular point of view to take you forward. So, whatever you aim to do—write a bestseller or just have the occasional or regular cheque to swell the holiday fund—be assured that you have to work at it. Furthermore, there are things you need to know and things you need to go about in the right way. Being persuasive is a case in point. Without thinking about it, the natural tendency is to stress, perhaps to interminably stress, what *you* see as the good things about your suggestion or your writing. As we have seen (in Chapter 3) there is an art to this and the key is not to think about you but about the editor, not to think about "me getting published", but about whether, and how, what you offer will help the editor you submit it to. And bear in mind that they will take a primarily commercial view of it; perhaps an exclusively commercial view of it.

The right approach can reverse your fortunes. Consider an example which shows very simply how getting the way you put things right can make a pitch.

The television series, *Star Trek* is now a legend across the globe. The original series may have started slowly, but it gained cult status, spawned several spin-off series across many years and led to a long series of successful films, one revitalised yet again recently. Financially it is one of the most successful such franchises ever. Yet it may be difficult, 30 odd years on, to remember how different it was at its inception from other programmes broadcast at the time. Gene Roddenberry had to find a way of pitching his programme idea to the networks: he thought he had a truly novel idea, and understandably he pushed the novelty and the difference with the passion of a creative originator. But initially in vain; despite his best efforts there were no takers.

Finally he realised that those he sought to persuade were essentially conservative and that many programmes accepted were actually close to something already existing—the classic known quantity; novelty could actually be off-putting.

One of the most successful television series at the time was the programme, *Wagon Train*—a western. But the circumstances of the characters, a tight-knit group, moving on to pastures new, and with each episode involving what happened to them in the new location and the people they met there, they were essentially similar to his idea for a space odyssey. He ultimately sold *Star Trek* by describing it in just four words... "*Wagon Train* in space". At the time this was a well-chosen analogy and people understood and, despite the risk of something so new and different, he got agreement to make the programme. And the rest, as they say, is history.

The moral is clear: by and large people want things that fit *their* mind set (they are less interested in why you may think it is good), and they are only persuaded when something offered *does* fit their situation—indeed the fact that it is offered as a good fit is itself an encouragement, showing that the writer understands both sides of the matter and making a positive decision more likely.

The rewards of getting it right are considerable. Many people like the opportunity to work at home, to be flexible, to have the satisfaction of writing and of getting some payment for it (at whatever level may be your target). Of course the range of writing that is possible—from a novel to a one-off, technical article—is wide and so are the possible benefits. Let me give you just one, personal, example. A year or two back, I had a light-hearted book of travel writing published. Titled, *Beguiling Burma*, it recorded a journey through Burma, mainly along the river (see www.patrickforsyth. com). This was a quite expensive trip to set up and the book was unlikely to ever make me a fortune, though I am now into profit, certainly if I include talks I give about my writing and my travel writing in particular. But I had the experience. I made the journey and I was introduced to a wonderful country I would probably never have seen without wearing a writer's hat. The potential return from writing is not just financial and this example had non-financial rewards in plenty. The same principle can apply to many different kinds of writing and project in a plethora of different ways. Just getting a letter published in a magazine may get you a prize.

So the theme here of making a return from your writing extends far. Doing so successfully is not, as I believe I have made clear, made possible by one simple magic formula. More's the pity! Success, which certainly is possible, comes from the details and particularly from a mindset that accepts that a constant chain of thinking, ideas and action must become part of your life. Your strike rate is never going to be 100 percent (if it is, well done and please tell me how!). So you always need new ideas and new action to carry you forward.

Such a process always reminds me of a classic tale…

…in medieval times there was a servant in the King's household who was condemned to life imprisonment for some small misdemeanour. Languishing in his cell, a thought struck him and he sent a message to the King promising that, if he were released, he would work day and night and, within a year, he would teach the King's favourite horse to talk.

This amused the King, and he ordered the servant to be released to work in the Royal stables. The servant's friends were at once pleased to see him released, yet frightened for him too; after all horses do not talk, however much training they get. "What will you do?" they all asked. "So much can happen in a year," he replied. "I may die, the King may die, or—who knows—the horse may talk!"

Who knows indeed; I for one hope that, by the time the year was up, he had thought of another ruse. And surely this is no bad thing to have in mind as you press "Save", pause in your writing and make yourself turn to considering what you can do next to ensure another cheque drops through the letter box. It may be a never-ending process, but it has been my intention that, next time you do this, ideas will come just a little more easily. Finally, I will not end by wishing you good luck, this may help occasionally but, as we have seen, it cannot be relied upon—but I do wish you well with it.

Index

More titles for the Creative Writer

Writing Science Fiction 'What if…!'

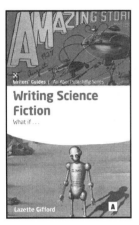

Who else wants to write science fiction?
Written by professional writer (see www.lazette.net/) this book takes the reader by the hand and explains exactly how to create a commercially successful science fiction novel. The author is well known in the genre and regularly teaches creative writing. This book defines science fiction and explains the different categories of science fiction. The reader is then taught the basics of research, how to build a world based on science and myth, how to build 'the others', namely building up believable characters in your Aliens, how to write the language of the future, placing stories in the universe, space travel, the possibilities of government in the future, the challenge of writing something new, creating an effective outline, being a professional writer and preparing your manuscript for the publisher.

Lazette Gifford is a name in science fiction circles. She lives with her husband and family in the USA where she is a prolific writer, photographer and computer generated artist.

Author Lazette Gifford | **Price** £10.99 €12.99 | **Format** Paperback, 215 x 135mm, 160pp

ISBN 978-1-84285-060-2

Kate Walker's 12 Point Guide to Writing Romance

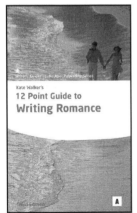

Here is how to become a published romance writer
If you want to write romance and be a professional writer then this book is a must for you. Following on from the success of the first edition of this book, which won a major award, this guide explains what is meant by romance and takes you through the process of writing emotion and conflict. The author explains how dialogue should be natural between your heroine and her hero and she explains the difference between sensuality and passion. With an expanded text and more true insider-secrets this is a must for all writers of romance, whether professional or amateur.
In this book you will learn:
• How to write emotion and create PTQ (page turning quality).
• Why dialogue is the lifeblood of your novel.
• The importance of 'after'.
• Why the intense black moment is so important.

Kate Walker has published in over 50 countries and has sold over 15 million romance novels worldwide.

Author Kate Walker | **Price** £10.99 €12.99 | **Format** Paperback, 215 x 135mm, 160pp

ISBN 978-1-84285-128-9

Writing Historical Fiction -

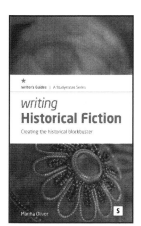

Creating the historical blockbuster
Who else wants to become a top selling novelist?
Have you always wanted to write historical fiction but not known
how to go about it? Or are you a published novelist who wants to
switch genres? In her meticulously researched book – packed with
worked examples, summaries and tips - Marina Oliver covers all
aspects of writing historical fiction –
This book includes details on:
• ten things you need to do to get started
• how to research your target period
• presenting your work to a publisher or agent
• the 5 stages of a plot
• how to write convincing dialogue
• the publication process

Marina Oliver has published over 50 historical novels and is a well-
known teacher of creative writing.

Author Marina Oliver | **Foreword** Richard Lee Founder of the Historical Novel Society
Price £10.99 €12.99 | **Format** Paperback, 215 x 135mm, 160pp

ISBN 978-1-84285-077-0

Writing 'how-to' articles and books

How to share your know-how and get published
Here is how to be a successful non-fiction writer
Who else wants to use their knowledge and experience to write non-
fiction articles and books?
It really could be you! Just imagine, with a little bit of guidance you
really could have your book on the bookshelves of national and even
international chains of bookshops. This book will show you how to
achieve it.
In this book Chris McCallum explains how to:
• Assess your knowledge and experience.
• Write 'how-to' articles.
• Write for magazines.
• Survive and succeed in today's publishing world.
• Break in with tips and fillers.
• Approach your market.
• Write a 'how-to' book.

Chriss Mc Callum has over 30 years of experience in the book trade both as a writer and as a publishing
executive.

Author Chriss McCallum | **Price** £10.99 €12.99 | **Format** Paperback, 215 x 135mm, 240pp

ISBN 13 978-1-84285-095-4

Writing Crime Fiction -

Making Crime Pay
Information Points
• Written by an expert who is a published crime writer
• Deals with a growing market of amateurs and undergraduates
• Each chapter develops a mental or practical skill
• Advice packaged in bite-sized chunks.

Here is how to become a published crime writer
Writing crime is an excellent introduction to
the genre from a well-established and
highly respected author.

In this book you will learn:
• How to start writing crime
• How to layer your novel with clues
• How to find a market for your work
• How to be a professional crime writer

Foreword by
International
Best-selling author
Val McDermid

Janet Laurence is an established crime writer. She is the author of the *Darina Lisle* crime series and the *Canaletto* murder series and the novel *To Kill the Past*. She is also the writer in residence at a college in Australia every summer. Janet Laurence lives in Somerset where like her heroine she enjoys cooking.

Author Janet Laurence | **Price** £10.99 €12.99 | **Format** Paperback, 215 x 135mm, 160pp

ISBN 13 978-1-84285-088-6

Starting to Write: Step-by-step guidance to becoming an author

Information Points
• Written by an expert academic who is also a published writer
• Deals with a growing market of amateurs and undergraduates
• Each chapter develops a mental or practical skill
• Advice packaged in bite-sized chunks.

Here is how to become a published writer
Many people yearn to become a published writer but publishers
complain of the poor quality manuscripts they receive and how they
are un-publishable. There are a substantial number of novice writers
who are making totally avoidable mistakes.
In this book you will learn:
• How to start writing and become your best critic
• How to deal with writers block, rejection and still keep writing
• How to find a market for your work
• How to find the best writing style and best area to write in, for your
  personality.

Chriss Mc Callum has over 30 years of experience in the book trade both as a writer and as a publishing executive.

Author Dr Rennie Parker | **Price** £10.99 €12.99 | **Format** Paperback, 215 x 135mm, 160pp

ISBN 978-184285-093-0

Writing and Imagery

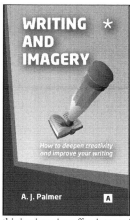

How to deepen creativity and improve your writing

Information Points
• Creative writing is one of the fastest-growing reader groups in the UK.
• Potential to market through the network of writers' groups and specialist writing press.
• Author is a 'name' in creative writing, regularly leads creative writing classes and is credited with finding a new talent Mark Lawrence of Prince of Thorns.

Here is how to use creativity to improve your writing
Written by professional writer and very experienced creative writing teacher, this book explains the nature of creativity and how a basic understanding of the brain function can enhance the creative process. This book explains how through cultural shifts, the use of imagery has become more mainstream in the last 25-years and how this is a jumping off point to using creative imagery to reframe writing for different markets.

Author Ann Palmer | **Price** £10.99 €12.99 | **Format** Paperback, 215 x 135mm, 160pp

ISBN 978-1-84285-061-9

Writing Soap: How to write Continuous Drama

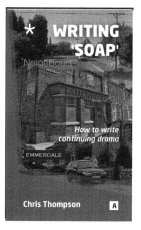

Information Points
• Authoritative - written by a very experienced radio and tv writer
• A growing market of creative writers ready to snap up this book.
• Huge market- there are many thousands of novice creative writers in the UK alone

Who else wants to write for the 'soaps'?
'Soaps' like *Eastenders, Coronation Street, Emmerdale, Casualty, Holby City*, and of course the ever-popular *Archers* on BBC Radio 4 all need new storylines to keep them fresh and that means new writers. It really could be your lines being uttered by an actor in a scene on tv or radio.

This book explains how:
• continuous drama is made and the role of the script writer
• to write for established characters in a 'soap'
• to develop your writing style so that it becomes compelling writing

Author Chris Thompson | **Price** £11.99 €12.99 | **Format** Paperback, 215 x 135mm, 160pp

ISBN 13 978-1-84285-118-0